WE'VE GOT YOUR NUMBER

Mukul Patel

Illustrated by Supriya Sahai

KINGFISHER

NEW YORK

KINGFISHER
LONDON & NEW YORK

Copyright © Kingfisher 2013
Published in the United States by Kingfisher,
175 Fifth Ave., New York, NY 10010
Kingfisher is an imprint of Macmillan Children's Books, London.
All rights reserved.

Created for Kingfisher by Brown Bear Books Ltd.
Original concept: Brown Bear Books Ltd.

Distributed in the U.S. and Canada by Macmillan, 175 Fifth Ave., New York, NY 10010

Library of Congress Cataloging-in-Publication data has been applied for.

ISBN: 978-0-7534-7072-5

Kingfisher books are available for special promotions and premiums.
For details contact: Special Markets Department, Macmillan,
175 Fifth Ave., New York, NY 10010.

For more information, please visit www.kingfisherbooks.com

Printed in China
1 3 5 7 9 8 6 4 2
1TR/0413/WKT/UG/128MA

PICTURE CREDITS
The Publisher would like to thank the following for permission to reproduce their material. Every care has been taken to trace copyright holders. However, if there have been unintentional omissions or failure to trace copyright holders, we apologize and will, if informed, endeavor to make corrections in any future edition.

Interior: Getty Images: Zachery T. Jensen 39c; **istockphoto:** 89; **NASA:** GRIN 91; **Public Domain:** 17br, 21, 37; **Robert Hunt Library:** 27, 52, 90: **Science Photo Library:** 31; **Shutterstock:** Bennyartist 64b, Yuriy Boyko 69, Alexey Bragin 64–65, Sandra Caldwell 53, Concept 51, Coprid 64–65, Claudio Divizia 35, Mikele Dray 56, Georgios Kollidas 42b, Eduard Kyzlynzky 54, Nagel Photography 54, M. Panchenko 45bl, 45bru, 85, Ingram Publishing 40r, istockphoto 17bc, 40, 45br, 83, Photosobjects.net 39t, Photos.com 46; **Topfoto:** 70, The Granger Collection 76.
All artwork: Brown Bear Books Ltd.

Brown Bear Books Ltd. has made every attempt to contact the copyright holders. If anyone has any information, please contact smortimer@windmillbooks.co.uk

CONTENTS

WHAT IS MATHEMATICS?

What is mathematics? Well, it's certainly not just addition or subtraction or even long division. It's not a science, though all science depends on it. Math is more like an art. And it's very much a living subject, with a continual stream of new discoveries, inventions, ideas, and applications.

We get the word "mathematics" from the Greek *mathema*, meaning knowledge. Arithmetic, geometry, and algebra are important parts of mathematics, but an overall description of what math is would be something like "making and playing with patterns." The 19th-century polymath (all-around expert) Henri Poincaré described mathematics as the "art of giving the same name to different things." When you figure out which of a set of things belong together, and give them a name, you're making a pattern.

PAGE NUMBERS

You'll notice something unusual about the page numbers in this book. Every page has its ordinary number in our decimal counting system, which is based on the numbers 0 to 9. But base 10—our counting system—is not the only way of counting. So we've also put the page numbers in base 16, or hexadecimal, which is used in computers (as you'll see on pages 14–15). "Hex" uses the symbols 0 to 9 but also uses A, B, C, D, E, and F. 1B in hex, for example, is 1 x 16 plus 1 x 11 = 27.

Science or art?

Carl Friedrich Gauss, who was called the "prince of mathematicians," described math as the "queen of sciences." But is math really a science? In science, experiments and evidence suggest theories that suggest experiments and so on. In math, although experiments and evidence are useful, in the end, they don't count for much—what you need is absolute proof. You can only prove something by reasoning logically from an agreed starting point. Creating such proofs is a lot like drawing an intricate map or pattern. And just because there's logic involved doesn't mean there's only one way to make an argument.

Try this at home

The best way to discover the beauty of math is to try it for yourself. Look for "Try this at home" boxes that contain questions for you to think about. Don't worry—it's not a test. The problems are designed to show you the kind of things mathematicians think about and the ways in which they think about them. If you get stuck, the solutions are listed on page 92. Or why not get involved with some research? The Internet allows large-scale collaboration—crowdsourcing—and some theorems have been proved by lots of people, including students, working together. One project that you can help with without needing to know much math is the Great Internet Mersenne Prime Number Search, a hunt for large primes. Tomorrow's mathematicians are growing up now—who's to say you won't be one of them? And that might be true even if you find math tough. Einstein found it hard, too!

Do I have to?

> *"Clouds are not spheres, mountains are not cones, coastlines are not circles, and bark is not smooth, nor does lightning travel in a straight line."*
> BENOIT MANDELBROT (1924–2010)

> *"Every good mathematician is at least half a philosopher, and every good philosopher is at least half a mathematician."*
> FRIEDRICH LUDWIG GOTTLOB FREGE (1848–1925)

Poincaré called math an "art" because doing math is not just about following a set of rules to get to an answer: You have to create, explore, juggle with, and even battle with ideas. Mathematicians are like painters, adventurers, acrobats, and knights, all rolled into one. And if you ask a mathematician what he or she is really looking for, he or she is likely to say something like "beauty" or "elegance."

What mathematicians do

Mathematicians are people who find mathematical patterns everywhere: in tree branches and soap bubbles, music and architecture, and even in bus routes. Among other things, mathematicians describe how climates change and how hair blows in the wind.

> *"Mathematics is a game played according to certain rules with meaningless marks on paper."*
> DAVID HILBERT (1862–1943)

Discovery or invention?

Is math discovered or invented? Theorems in math are always true, everywhere: Pythagoras's theorem works just as well in China as in Greece, and it was discovered from scratch in both places and many others as well. But people invent different ways of doing math. Ancient Chinese mathematicians were great problem solvers, while the ancient Greeks were really into proving ideas and looking for beauty. So even though mathematical theorems seem to be "out there" somewhere, waiting to be discovered, people invent their own routes (and sometimes entire landscapes) to reach them.

SEQUENCES

One important idea in math is the idea of a sequence, or a list of numbers in some order. Each chapter of *We've Got Your Number* features a sequence of numbers that are related to each other in a particular way. Can you figure out the patterns? There's a hint on each chapter opener to help you—and the answers are all in the back.

They observe how plants grow and water flows, make and break secret codes, and guide spacecraft to distant planets. They know about ways of tying shoelaces and what to charge for a plane ticket. And they're experts on infinity! Although really understanding an idea is something that you can only do on your own, mathematicians often work with others: mathematicians and physicists, but also engineers, zoologists, computer programmers, neurosurgeons, city planners—even fashion designers!

In the following pages, you'll get a glimpse of what mathematics really is: a multicolored, bizarre, and beautiful creature that you can find in the smallest corners and the farthest reaches of our universe.

Horse or donkey? It's all relative!

Proof

FROM
HERE TO
INFINITY

HINT!

(Pages 10–19) It's about its position in the sequence .
(Pages 20–31) It's all in the shape.

Mathematical theorems (a theorem is a true statement, such as there is no largest prime number) are true forever. Math, on the other hand, is a relatively young subject. It's only been around for about 2,500 years—but it is growing at an incredible rate. All of the mathematics that was known 100 years ago would have fitted into about 100 big books. Today, you'd need 100,000 books to hold what we know! But there's no shortage of questions left to solve. Lots of them are new, but some are hundreds of years old.

Ancient mathematicians worked mostly with numbers and counting—except for the Greeks, who were more interested in geometry and shapes. In Asia, math was used to solve practical problems. Later, when Islamic culture was at its richest in the Middle Ages, ideas from East and West met, and methods such as algebra were developed. Europe became a center for math from around the 17th century, and today, math keeps people busy all over the world.

COUNTING THE COSMOS

Tallying is a slow way to count.

Counting started in prehistoric times as a way to solve problems such as keeping track of things. Over generations, people separated the way of counting from the things being counted.

About 35,000 years ago, humans counted by scratching tally marks in bones. Perhaps they were counting the animals they'd hunted or how many times they saw the full moon. But tallying is slow. It's like counting using only the digit 1. To count 20 things, you had to make 20 separate marks.

Numbers arrive

That changed about 10,000 years ago, when farming began in Mesopotamia (modern-day Iraq). Farmers had to keep track of the seasons, mark out their fields, and count their crops—they didn't have time to tally. The Sumerians of Mesopotamia developed symbols for groups of tally marks: They wrote 1 as ⟨symbol⟩, 9 as ⟨symbol⟩, and 10 as ⟨symbol⟩.

This was the beginning of abstraction. Now people could count a set of objects using symbols that stood for numbers, not a mark for each object.

Understanding the cosmos

Counting objects soon led to practical developments, such as measuring and

Life's too short to tally.

The Sumerians wrote numbers and words by pressing shapes into clay.

Ways of counting

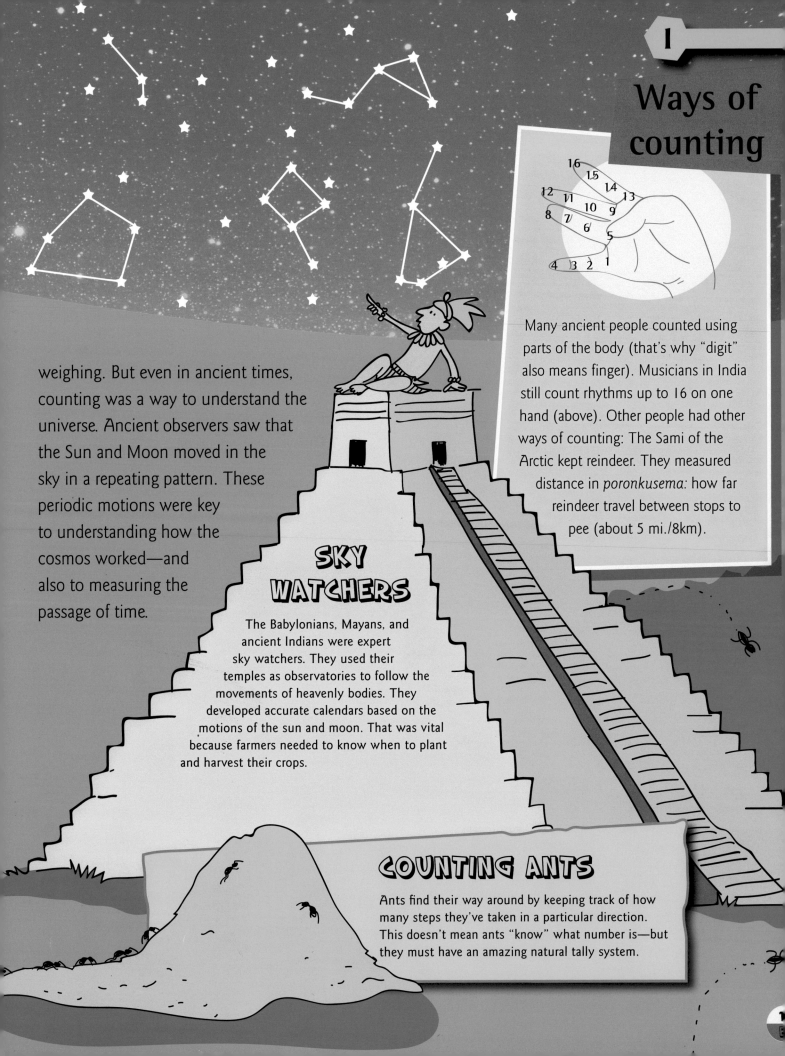

Many ancient people counted using parts of the body (that's why "digit" also means finger). Musicians in India still count rhythms up to 16 on one hand (above). Other people had other ways of counting: The Sami of the Arctic kept reindeer. They measured distance in *poronkusema*: how far reindeer travel between stops to pee (about 5 mi./8km).

weighing. But even in ancient times, counting was a way to understand the universe. Ancient observers saw that the Sun and Moon moved in the sky in a repeating pattern. These periodic motions were key to understanding how the cosmos worked—and also to measuring the passage of time.

SKY WATCHERS

The Babylonians, Mayans, and ancient Indians were expert sky watchers. They used their temples as observatories to follow the movements of heavenly bodies. They developed accurate calendars based on the motions of the sun and moon. That was vital because farmers needed to know when to plant and harvest their crops.

COUNTING ANTS

Ants find their way around by keeping track of how many steps they've taken in a particular direction. This doesn't mean ants "know" what number is—but they must have an amazing natural tally system.

THE NUMBER LINE

Did someone say pie?

When you think of numbers, you might think of whole numbers such as 1 or 43. You might think of negative numbers such as -1 or -13. But that's only part of the story.

For one thing, there's an infinity of numbers: in both directions. Imagine that the natural (whole) numbers, such as 1, 2, 3, and so on, are marked on a line that stretches to ∞ (infinity). Add zero and then the negative whole numbers to its left. We've made a number line that stretches forever in both directions, from – ∞ to ∞. Okay, it's a very long line. BUT, now every possible number should exist somewhere on it. Or does it?

The answer is, not even close. There's an infinite number of fractions to squeeze in between 0 and 1: just keep halving a half. But you can also divide ¹/₃ into thirds. That's infinite infinities before we've gotten past 1!

THIS WAY TO
-∞

-4310675647 -21,129 -1,329

-585

-126.33

USEFUL TOOLS

Ancient Indian and Chinese mathematicians tried to solve everyday problems, not to try to understand the universe. They had no problem using negative numbers—say, to represent the debts someone was owed.

-17 0

0 ... 9/3178 ... 1/4 ... 28/100 ... 1/2 ... 201/400 ... 2/3 ... 3/4

An infinity of fractions fits between 0 and 1 ... and between all the other whole numbers.

1

ICONIC NUMBER

Pi (π), the ratio of a circle's circumference to its diameter, is an irrational number: You can approximate it as ²²/₇, or ³⁵⁵/₁₁₃, or 3.14159, but it's impossible to write exactly as a fraction or decimal number. Pi turns up wherever there are circles, but also wherever there are angles. People have calculated the first 10 *trillion* digits of π, though for most purposes—such as designing a building or sending a spacecraft to Mars—a few digits is enough!

Yum!

THIS WAY TO ∞

8375020573537S827

9016479289381

89,479,289,50

897.52   75,953   9,647,353

167.9

35.7

5

2

The spaces between the rational numbers are home to irrational numbers.

Irrational numbers

But there are STILL gaps in the line. What's missing are the irrational numbers such as π (irrational numbers are not crazy: They just can't be written as fractions, and as decimals, they go on forever without repeating). Between any two rational numbers on the line, you can find an irrational number. That's a lot of irrational numbers. And between any two irrational numbers, you can find a rational number, which is a lot of rational numbers. It's only once we add the irrationals in that we end up with the complete number line. Phew!

NUMBER BASES

We're used to counting based on the number 10. The decimal system uses tens, hundreds, thousands, millions, and so on. But it didn't have to be this way. If we had fewer fingers, we might count everything in base 8!

In positional number systems, the value of a digit depends on where it is in a number. The digit 1 in the number 10, for example, means something different than it does in the number 100. The base of a positional system is the number of different digits it uses. For instance, the decimal system uses the 10 digits from 0 to 9, so its base is 10. This tells us that each place (column) of a number is worth 10 times as much as the one to its right.

BASED IN BABYLON

We organize units of time (minutes and seconds), geographic coordinates (degrees, minutes, and seconds of latitude and longitude), and angles (degrees, minutes, and seconds) in multiples of 60. This comes from the ancient Babylonian number system, which used a form of base 60, or sexagesimal.

Covering the bases

Our world still has traces of other number systems. We buy eggs by the dozen and divide the year into 12 months. These divisions come from number systems that used different number bases. Ancient peoples based counting systems on 5 (quinary), 6 (senary), 8 (octal), 12 (duodecimal), and even 20 (vigesimal). Base 4 (quartenary) was popular because it was the number of legs a cow had. Binary (base 2) and hexadecimal, or hex (base 16), are still used in computing.

I think my calculator's broken ...

Numbers for computers

In base 2, there are just two digits (called bits, from **b**inary dig**its**), 0 and 1. The columns in a number are values of powers of 2:

8	4	2	1
1	0	0	1

$$
\begin{aligned}
& 1 \times 1 \\
+\ & 0 \times 2 \\
+\ & 0 \times 4 \\
+\ & 1 \times 8 \\
=\ & 9 \text{ in decimal.}
\end{aligned}
$$

Having just two symbols means that binary numbers can be represented by any system with two distinct states, such as an electrical circuit being on or off. Binary numbers are how digital computers represent data—because computers are really just networks of millions of on–off switches.

The disadvantage of binary is that large numbers need many bits to write. For 1,025, you need 11 bits: 100 0000 0001. That's where hexadecimal comes in. It's easy to turn binary numbers into hex numbers because the base of hex, 16, is a power of 2, which is the base of binary. Hex has 16 symbols: 0–9, plus the letters A, B, C, D, E, and F, which represent 10, 11, 12, 13, 14, and 15.

You need fewer symbols to write large numbers in hex than in decimal, and far fewer than in binary. For instance, the 5-digit hex number F462B requires 7 digits in decimal (1,001,003) and 20 in binary: 1111 0100 0110 0010.

Showing the bases

To show what base you're using, you can add a subscript: So 100_2 is 100 in binary, which equals 4 in decimal (4_{10}). For any base b, 10_b is one b and zero units. So 10_2 (binary) is 2 (decimal), and 10_{16} (in hex) is 16 (decimal).

Try this at home:
Think like a computer

It's easy to convert between binary and hex. Every hex digit can be written as a group of 4 bits. If you know the binary equivalent for the 16 hex (base 16) digits, the conversion becomes very fast; F3 is 1111 0011, because $F_{16} = 1111_2$ and $3_{16} = 0011_2$.

Hmmm ... This isn't really working ...

NOTHING, NADA, NIL, ZERO

There's NOTHING in here!!

Don't put first things first: Put zeroth things zeroth. You may think zero has always been around— but you'd be wrong.

Zero represents nothing. That sounds simple, but can you think of nothing? Try to think of no oranges. Is it the same as not thinking of any oranges? The idea that nothing could be counted —which meant it must be something—was a hot topic for the ancient Greeks.

Early number systems didn't include zero. But as long ago as 3000 B.C., the Babylonians began using a positional number system.

Nor here ...

Try this at home
Prove that 2=1

The special qualities of zero make the impossible possible. Take the equations $1 \times 0 = 0$ and $2 \times 0 = 0$. Therefore $1 \times 0 = 2 \times 0$. Divide both sides by zero, so all the zeros cancel out. You're left with $1 = 2$. Use this equation to wow your friends ... and your math teacher!

Meet zero ...

Zero lies in the middle of the number line, with the other numbers racing off toward infinity in both directions. It is an even integer (like 2 or –2), but neither positive nor negative. Zero is the identity for addition: When you add it to a number, that number remains unchanged. Any number multiplied by zero is zero, but division by zero still poses a problem. An early suggestion was that dividing by zero gives infinity, but today, we call division by zero "undefined." If we were to allow it in arithmetic, then we'd also have to admit that 1 = 2. And you can see where that would lead ...

What zero does
$$5 \times 0 = 0$$
$$5 - 0 = 5$$
$$5 + 0 = 5$$
$$5 \div 0 = ???!!$$

The value of a number depended on both the digit (such as "0" or "1") and its position in a string of digits. The early Babylonians counted in base 60. They left a space where we would write 0 in a string. Later, they replaced the gap with a placeholder symbol: That's the role "0" plays today in a number like 101.

A question of division

The earliest evidence for zero being used as a number comes from India in about A.D. 600. Indian thinkers could add, subtract, and multiply numbers including zero. But they couldn't agree on what dividing by zero might mean.

The Mayans of Central America came up with the same idea. But it was from India that the idea of zero spread around the world.

BRAHMAGUPTA

One of the first people to use zero as a number was the 7th-century Indian scholar Brahmagupta, who studied problems in geometry and algebra. The idea of zero only spread to Europe in the 12th and 13th centuries, via Muslim scholars.

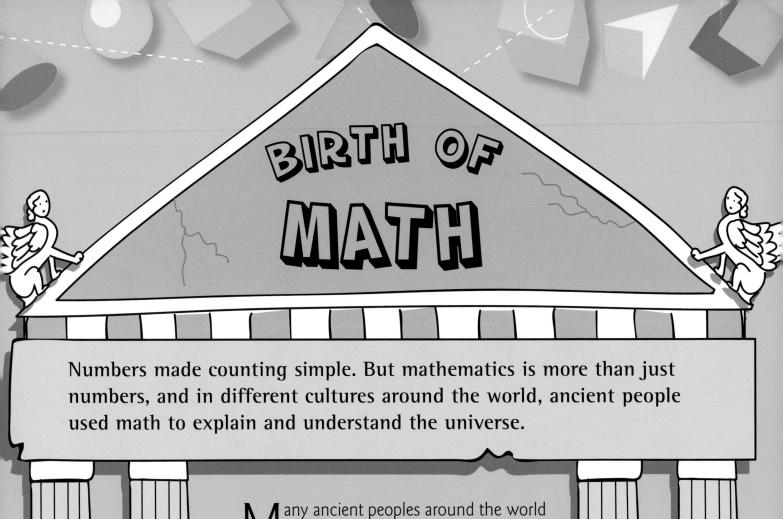

BIRTH OF MATH

Numbers made counting simple. But mathematics is more than just numbers, and in different cultures around the world, ancient people used math to explain and understand the universe.

Many ancient peoples around the world explored numbers. Some developed very advanced techniques for calculation —the Chinese figured out a very accurate value of π, for example. But the ancient Greeks were the A-Team of mathematics. Greek thinkers were unique for two reasons: First, they studied numbers and shapes for their own sake, and second, they figured out methods to prove, or test, their ideas. They saw math as being essential to understanding the world. The word *mathematics* comes from the ancient Greek word for "learning."

$(a+b)^2 = a^2 + 2ab + b^2$

$a^2 + b^2 = c^2$

Euclid

Euclid (325–265 B.C.) wrote down Greek mathematical knowledge down in 13 books. He set the method on which all mathematics is still based: He proved theorems using the rules of logic.

Pythagoras's theorem

The most famous theorem in math is named after the Greek Pythagoras. A theorem is a statement that has been proved. In the sixth century B.C., Pythagoras said that, in a right-angled triangle, the area of the square of the hypotenuse (the longest side) equals the sum of the area of the squares of the other two sides.

Pythagoras and his followers thought the universe was based on numbers. Pythagoras declared that "All is number." He said everything was made up of multiples of units, and any two measurements could be written as ratios of units, such as $1/2$ or $3/4$. (Although one of Pythagoras's followers discovered irrational numbers, which can't be written exactly as a ratio.)

I pi with my little eye.

A famous theorem

The theorem named after Pythagoras was known in other cultures. It was probably the Chinese who came up with this way to prove it visually. Take four copies of any right-angled triangle and arrange them like this in a large square, leaving an empty square of area c^2. Rearranging the triangles gives you two empty squares (a^2 and b^2). These two areas must be the same as the area of the single square, so $a^2 + b^2 = c^2$ where c is the hypotenuse of the right-angled triangle.

It's all Greek to me!

ARCHIMEDES OF SYRACUSE

(282–212 B.C.)

Archimedes was a scientist, but he also made huge contributions to mathematics. He developed ways of working with very large numbers, which allowed him to estimate the number of grains of sand that would fill the universe. He also found exact formulae for the areas and volumes of circles, cones, and spheres, and quite a good approximation for π.

UNFEASIBLY LARGE NUMBERS ... 1234567 89000000000000000000

Very large numbers are common in mathematics and science, but they don't often have special names. One name—the googol—was invented to show the difference between numbers that are just very big and infinity.

Mathematicians don't have names for most large numbers. Instead, they have ways of writing them, using factorials or powers, that need very few symbols. That's useful, since huge numbers are a pain to write. If a number is large enough, not only might it be impossible to write it out in a single person's lifetime—it might not even fit into our universe!

Iconic number
Googol

The word "googol" was invented by a nine-year-old boy who was asked by his mathematician uncle to think of a name for the number that's 1 followed by 100 zeros: 10,000,000,000,000,000,000,000, 000,000,000,000,000,000,000,000,000, 000,000,000,000,000,000,000,000,000, 000,000,000,000,000,000,000,000. Using powers of 10, we can write 1 googol as 10^{100}. It's such a big number, it has very few uses. But if that's still not big enough for you, how about a googolplex? That's 10^{googol}, or 1 followed by a googol zeros. Don't even think about trying to write out that number: There aren't enough atoms in the universe to do it! (So there isn't really anything we can count with a googolplex!) And it's still tiny compared to infinity.

FACTORIALS
24 = 4! The exclamation mark doesn't mean anyone is shouting. It means "factorial," or "multiply this number by the smaller positive integers." So 4! = $4 \times 3 \times 2 \times 1 = 24$, Factorials are useful to figure out ways to choose or arrange things, such as cards in a deck. The numbers get very large very quickly.

POWER TOWERS
For truly huge numbers, you can make a tower of powers: $10^{10} = 10,000,000,000$, but $10^{10^{10}}$ is 1 followed by 10 trillion zeros. 10^{googol} can also be written as $10^{10^{100}}$. You can just keep stacking up the powers. When figuring out towers of powers, you calculate the upper stories first.

Don't get paid in old Zimbabwe dollars:
A trillion wouldn't buy you a drink!

Try this at home

When you discuss your allowance, suggest this to your parents. They put 1¢ on the first square of a chessboard, 2¢ on the second square, 4¢ on the third, doubling until they reach the last square. They could be in for a surprise.

How about bigger pockets?

Astronomical ancient numbers

An ancient Indian text describes how the Buddha counted powers of 10 to 10^{421}, or 1 followed by 421 zeros. The biggest number the ancient Greeks used was a myriad (10,000). When the Greek thinker Archimedes estimated the number of grains of sand that would fill the universe, he multiplied a myriad myriad (100 million) a myriad myriad times. This allowed him to handle numbers large enough to figure out his estimate: 10^{63} (1 followed by 63 zeros) grains of sand. And Archimedes' system could cope with numbers much larger even than that.

Exponents

If you make the allowance deal (above), what's in it for you? Well, by the 27th square, you'd be a millionaire with $2^{27} - 1$¢ $= \$1,342,177.27$. By the last square you'd have $2^{64} - 1$¢ $= \$184,467,440,737,095,516.15$. That's over $184 thousand trillion. (You might have to lend some back to your folks.) This is an example of exponentiation, or raising a number to a power x. That means multiplying a number by itself (x) times. So, $10^2 = 10 \times 10 = 100$ and $2^5 = 2 \times 2 \times 2 \times 2 \times 2 = 32$. One million is 10^6, a billion is 10^9, and a trillion is 10^{12}. There are more than 10^{13} cells in your body, and supercomputers can make 10^{16} calculations every second.

AN INFINITY OF INFINITIES

It's not a number and it's not a place. It's farther away than any number you can think of. You can't do normal arithmetic with it. It lies at each "end" of the (never-ending) number line, but also within the smallest section of it.

Perhaps the simplest definition of infinity (∞) is "unlimited." There is an unlimited, or infinite, number of *natural numbers* because there is no biggest natural number. (If you think you've found it, that's great. But now add 1). The ancient Greek, Zeno of Elea (c. 490–430 B.C.), was the first to discuss infinity in a mathematical way. He used paradoxes, which are statements that make no logical sense. Take the Achilles paradox. Achilles (very quick) has a race against a tortoise (very slow). Achilles gives the tortoise a headstart, but he runs twice as fast as the tortoise, so he should still win, right? But Zeno showed that, mathematically, Achilles could only ever catch up by running an infinite number of distances. What the …?

Of course, that's not what would actually happen. The key is that, even though Achilles has to run an infinite number of distances, the distances get smaller very quickly, and their sum is not infinite. So, in real life, the tortoise loses.

Zeno's paradox

At each stage, the gap between Achilles and the tortoise closes by half. So whenever Achilles reaches where the tortoise was, the tortoise has moved on.

1

1/2

1/4

Try this at home

Hilbert's hotel can actually accommodate an infinite number of new arrivals. Can you see how?

I'd like a room with a view.

WE'RE FULL! ∞ VACANCIES

HILBERT'S HOTEL

HILBERT'S HOTEL

David Hilbert imagined a hotel with an infinite number of rooms, numbered 1, 2, 3, and so on, with a guest in each room. The hotel is full, but if one more guest arrives at reception, it's no problem: They can still have their own room. Each guest moves to the next room, so the guest in room 1 moves to room 2, the one in room 2 moves to room 3, and so on. Since there is no limit to the number of rooms, each original guest still gets a room, leaving room 1 empty for the new guest!

Cantor's crazy counting

Georg Cantor (1845–1918) realized that there were an infinite number of infinities. Although some mathematicians thought he was crazy, others, such as David Hilbert, recognized that he had changed math forever.

Cantor saw that you could count infinitely big groups, or sets, with the (infinitely many) natural numbers. The sets were all of the same (infinite) size. He called this infinity a countable infinity, or aleph-null. He then showed that you couldn't count all the real numbers, even between 0 and 1. He called this bigger, uncountable infinity aleph-one.

Cantor then showed there are an infinite number of ever-larger infinities: aleph-null, aleph-one, aleph-two, aleph-three, and so on. No wonder people thought he was crazy!

Scales of infinity

Cantor showed that many of the infinitely large countable infinities are the same size. So there are as many natural numbers as there are even natural numbers or odd natural numbers, or Fibonacci numbers, or prime numbers, or multiples of 100. Now that's bizarre!

EVEN INTEGERS   ODD INTEGERS   POSITIVE FRACTIONS   NEGATIVE FRACTIONS   PRIMES   FIBONACCI NUMBERS

Cantor showed that all countable infinities are the same size.

THE PRIME NUMBERS

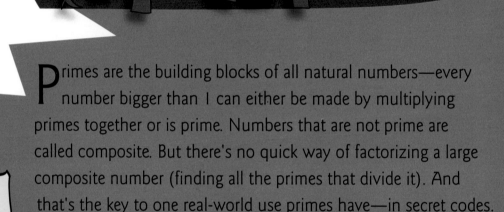

Prime numbers are numbers that can only be divided by 1 and themselves. They're the VIPs of the natural numbers. Primes fascinate mathematicians because they exhibit many puzzling patterns.

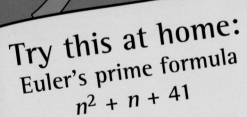

Try this at home: Euler's prime formula
$$n^2 + n + 41$$

This formula is a machine for making primes! For each natural number starting with 1, add it to its square and then add 41. For example, putting $n = 1$, $1^2 + 1 + 41 = 43$, which is a prime, and $n = 2$ gives 47, which is also a prime. How far can you go before the formula stops working?

Primes are the building blocks of all natural numbers—every number bigger than 1 can either be made by multiplying primes together or is prime. Numbers that are not prime are called composite. But there's no quick way of factorizing a large composite number (finding all the primes that divide it). And that's the key to one real-world use primes have—in secret codes.

If you do invent a quick way to factorize large numbers, keep it quiet! The codes that are used to keep communications secure online—including between banks—only work as long as no evil genius finds a quick algorithm for factorizing 200-digit numbers (not that you're an evil genius, of course …).

You're not on the list …

What, is it the shoes?

Sieve of Eratosthenes

Eratosthenes of Cyrene (c. 276–195 B.C.) found an algorithm to sieve out composites from a list, leaving only primes. Working up from 2, for every prime number, we delete its multiples starting from its square. For 2, we cross out 4, 6, 8 … and for 3, we cross out 9, 12, 15 … Since the list ends at 100 and 11^2 is bigger than 100, we can stop at 11. The numbers trapped by the sieve (left uncolored) are the primes less than 100.

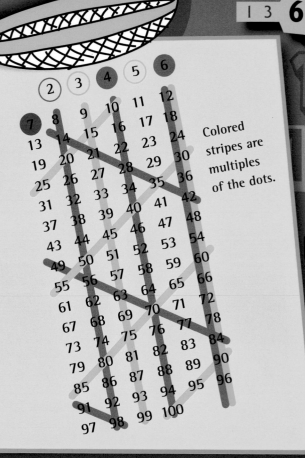

Colored stripes are multiples of the dots.

How large can you get?

Hunting for primes is a job for computers. Lots and lots of computers. Before computers, the largest known prime had 30 digits. Today, the largest known prime (in 2012) is $2^{43112609} - 1$, which has nearly 13 million digits! But don't stop there: Over 2,000 years ago, the Greek mathematician Euclid proved that you can always find a larger prime. Here's how he did it:

Suppose there is a largest prime (call it p). Then the primes in order of size are 2, 3, 5 … up to p. Multiply all these numbers together and then add 1. Call this number N.

Now, if N is prime, we've found a prime bigger than p. And if N is composite, then it is divisible by a prime between 1 and N. But this prime can't be in the list 2, 3, 5 … p, because we're left with a remainder of 1 when we divide N by any of those numbers. So again, we've found a prime bigger than p. And this argument works no matter how big p is!

We're out of paper again!

PRIME CUTS

- The smallest prime is 2, which is an odd prime—because it's the only even one! And the largest is …?
- There are infinitely many twin primes (primes that differ by 2, e.g. 41 and 43).
- You can always find a prime between a number bigger than 2 and its double, eg. between 3 and 6 you'll find the prime 5.
- You can find sequences (lists) of composites of any length you like. For example, there is a sequence of 13 composites from 114 to 126.

That's garbage!

IT'S A MOD-N WORLD

Wouldn't math be simpler if there weren't so many numbers? Say we got rid of all the irrational numbers and fractions. And all the negative numbers. And every number bigger than, say, 23? It might sound like cheating—but it's not.

Doing modular arithmetic is like counting on a loop. Or like reading the hours on a clock that goes from 1 to 12 and then back to 1 again. (The math is simpler if the clock starts from 0, like a 24-hour clock that goes to 23 and then back to 0.)

So what actually happens when you count in a loop? Well, suppose a 24-hour clock shows it's 21:00. What time will it be eight hours later? How did you get to 5:00? In your head, you added 8 and 21 to get 29, then looked at the remainder when you divided by 24. But if you write that as an equation, it looks a little odd:

$$21 + 8 = 5$$

Modular mathematics was pioneered by the Swiss mathematician Leonard Euler in the mid-18th century. It is sometimes called clock arithmetic, because when counting reaches a particular number, called the modulus, it wraps back to the start.

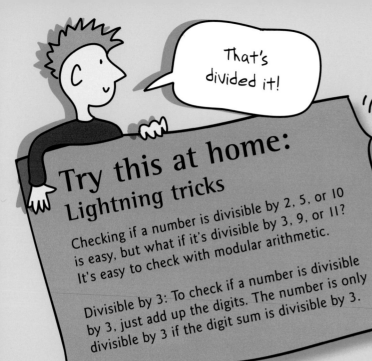

That's divided it!

Try this at home: Lightning tricks

Checking if a number is divisible by 2, 5, or 10 is easy, but what if it's divisible by 3, 9, or 11? It's easy to check with modular arithmetic.

Divisible by 3: To check if a number is divisible by 3, just add up the digits. The number is only divisible by 3 if the digit sum is divisible by 3.

Divisible by 9: You can use the same method to test for divisibility by 9, checking if the digit sum is a multiple of 9.

Divisible by 11: Alternately, subtract and add the digits of the number, from right to left. The number is divisible by 11 if the result is congruent to 0 mod 11. For example, in the number 1089, $9 - 8 + 0 - 1 = 0$ mod 11, so 1089 is divisible by 11.

Counting on congruence

Mathematicians use the congruence symbol ≡ to show they're using modular arithmetic. $21 + 8 \equiv 5$ mod 24 means that $21 + 8$ "equals" 5 in the mod 24 world. The remainder when you divide $21 + 8$ by 24 is the same as when you divide 5 by 24 (it's 5). You can add or subtract multiples of 24 to find other numbers congruent to 5: −19 and 53 are both congruent to 5 mod 24. So if you're working in mod 24, you can replace any −19 or 29 or 53 (or so on) with a 5.

CARL GAUSS

Carl Friedrich Gauss (1777–1855) figured out modular arithmetic by the time he was 19. That was nothing. When his elementary school teacher asked him to add up all the numbers 1 to 100, he figured out in seconds to add the numbers as 50 equal pairs (1 + 100, 2 + 99, etc.). The "prince of mathematics" didn't always publish his ideas, so other people get the credit for discoveries he made.

Using mods

You can easily add, subtract, multiply, and raise to powers in the mod-n world. But since you only work with remainders, the numbers are smaller, and the calculations are much easier than in normal math. (And, of course, you can count in loops of any length you like.) When you count in 7s (0, 1, 2, 3, 4, 5, 6, 0, 1, 2 …), you're doing mod 7 arithmetic.

What's the use of that?

Modular arithmetic has many uses. One is in "checksums" in barcodes and other kinds of digital data such as MP3 music files. One digit of the barcode doesn't contain any information about the item. It's chosen so that all the digits add up to a particular number (in modular arithmetic). If the scanner doesn't get this sum, there was a problem during scanning.

SETS AND LOGIC

What's more basic than numbers? Well, in math, the real starting points are sets (collections of things, or elements) and logic (rules of thinking). Anything can be an element: a number, a color, even another set.

When listing the elements of a set, it doesn't matter what order you put them in. So the set S = {invisible, pink, unicorn} is the same as the set T = {pink, invisible, unicorn}. Both the sets have the same elements. All the elements of the set U = {invisible, pink} are in S, so U is "contained in S" and is called a subset of S. But the set V = {invisible, purple} is not a subset of S, since purple is not an element of S.

We love zebras.

A hat trick

Three people—A, B, and C (not their real names, obviously)—sit in a row, one behind the other. C can see both B and A ahead of her; B can see only A; A is in the front and can't see B or C. Now hats are taken from a bag that they all know contains three green and two orange hats. The hats are placed on the head of each person, without them seeing it. They are then asked in sequence—C, B, and A—if they know the color of their own hats. C says, "No." Then B says, "No." But A says, "Yes, it's …" What color is A's hat? And how did she know?

Join our set!

I don't think so ...

Modern logic is based on George Boole's study of words such as "and," "or," "if," and "then" that connect statements together. Boolean logic is used in digital computers: Processors contain switches in groups called logic gates. An AND gate followed by a NOT gate makes a NAND gate. A few million NAND gates make ... a computer. Mathematicians write logic using symbols instead of words—it's much more efficient.

Rules of thinking

VENN DIAGRAM
Drawing pictures of sets can be an easy way of figuring out some problems. Suppose that out of 21 people, 13 like zebras, 7 like rhinos, and 5 like both. How many like neither?

Many ancient cultures shared similar ideas about rules of thinking. The system of logic developed by the ancient Greek thinker Aristotle became the most widely used. His three basic rules still apply:

• Identity—A thing is the same as itself.
• Noncontradiction— A thing can't be and not be at the same time.
• The excluded middle—Either a statement is true or its opposite is true.

Using these rules, Aristotle developed a type of argument called a syllogism, in which from two statements we deduce (correctly make) a third. For example,
(1) All unicorns are pink.
(2) Some unicorns are invisible.
So, (3) some pink things are invisible.
It doesn't matter if the first two statements are actually true: We're only concerned about a pattern. If (1) and (2) are both true, then (3) must be true. But some syllogisms are invalid (incorrect), for example:
(1) All unicorns are pink.
(2) Some pink things are rhinos.
So, (3) some unicorns are rhinos.

I'm telling you, you're no UNICORN!

~~PRYTHE~~ ~~PROOTH~~ ~~PRUFE~~ PROOF ✓

To show that a mathematical statement is true, you have to argue from basic starting points called axioms. Some proofs are simple diagrams; others take dozens of mathematicians working over generations.

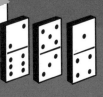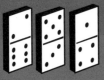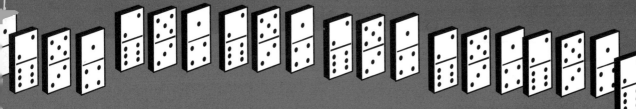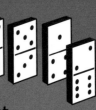

To prove that a statement is true, it can be easier to assume that it is actually false. This is known as proof by contradiction. If you use a logically correct argument, you'll reach a conclusion that is clearly absurd. Since your argument is correct, your assumption (that the statement is false) must be false, and so the statement must be true. You can use this kind of argument to prove, say, that there is no smallest positive number.

The domino effect

Proof by induction works like a domino chain, where a falling domino hits the next one and so on. If you push the first domino, the entire chain will topple. To prove that a formula works for all natural numbers, you first show that it if works for some number, x, then it also works for the next number. Now check if it works for the number 1. If so, then the first domino falls—and all the others after it.

What's the smallest positive number?

Okay. Now halve it.

I've got it! I've got it!

Drat!

Try this at home:
Counterexamples

You can't prove a statement by listing examples—you would need to show it was true for all cases. But you can disprove a statement, or show it's false, by finding a counterexample (an example that doesn't work). For example, can you disprove the statement: "All prime numbers are odd?"

YOU ARE HERE

Try this at home:
Four-color theorem

The four-color theorem says that it is possible to color any flat map with just four colors so that no regions that border each other are the same color (they may share a color if they only touch at a single corner, or point). Why not try? Photocopy this map of the United States, or find any other blank map that shows different states or counties or countries, and see if you can color it using only four colors.

KURT GÖDEL

In 1931, the Austrian logician Kurt Gödel (1906–1978) showed that there could be true theorems that you could not prove: not because it was too difficult to prove them, but because it was impossible. He also showed that you couldn't prove that the axioms you used wouldn't contradict each other. Luckily, mathematicians don't have to deal with these problems every day!

Proof by computer

A statement that seems to be true but has not yet been proven is called a conjecture. Once proven, it is called a theorem. One famous theorem is the four-color theorem. It says that you need at the most four colors to color in any map so that no bordering regions have the same color. There is a one-page proof that you don't need more than five colors, but no one has found a neat way of proving it for four. In 1976, two mathematicians did manage to prove it with the help of a computer. Other computers have checked the proof—but it would take humans way too long.

BIZARRE SHAPES, WEIRD SPACES

Ever since the ancient Greeks, the study of shape has been a major part of math. For the Greeks, geometry—the study of shapes and distances—came before everything else. Repeated patterns have been especially important in Islamic cultures, which only allow artists to paint abstract pictures. The medieval Islamic palace of the Alhambra in Granada, Spain, contains all the 17 possible basic tilings. Later, mathematicians discovered and invented some truly bizarre shapes, such as fractals, which can't be really appreciated without computer graphics.

It's not all about particular shapes. In the 17th century, Descartes took the brilliant step of combining algebra and geometry, and so invented the coordinate system. This paved the way for studying dimensions, especially higher dimensions (ever tried 4-dimensional tic-tac-toe?).

It's even possible to say lots of interesting things about shapes without talking about sizes. The branch of math called topology deals with shapes in this way. What's important is how shapes join together or whether they have holes or creases in them, not how large or small they are.

On a map, it's easy to tell where land ends and the sea begins. In real life, it's easy to tell, too: Your feet get wet, or you fall off a cliff. But a coastline is actually a very complicated shape.

HOW LONG IS A COASTLINE?

MANDELBROT'S COASTLINE

The Polish-born mathematician Benoit Mandelbrot coined the term fractal. It comes from the Latin word *fractus*, which means *broken* or *irregular*. In the 1950s, he began to explore different types of these repeating patterns. He even used them to predict changes in the prices of commodities.

It seems obvious that a coastline must have a fixed size, just as a square or a circle has a fixed perimeter. But with a shape like a coastline (or clouds or ferns), it depends on what you use for measuring. If you use a thick rope to measure a section of coastline, it won't go into all the nooks. If you use a thinner rope, it will —so the rope will be longer. And if you use the thinnest thread, it would need to be even longer.

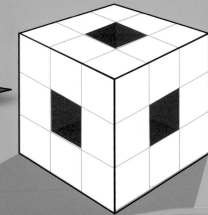

MENGER SPONGE
This fractal is a "solid" shape with zero volume and infinite surface area. To make one, divide a cube into 27 smaller cubes and remove the central cube on each side and in the middle. Then repeat the process for the smaller cubes.

Spain vs. Portugal

In the early 20th century, the British scientist L. F. Richardson studied borders between countries. He believed that the longer the border, the more likely the countries were to go to war. But when he looked at the border of Spain and Portugal, he got a surprise. Portugal is much smaller than Spain, so its maps show more detail. On Portuguese maps, therefore, the border appeared to be longer than on the less-detailed Spanish maps.

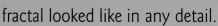

Fractals

Coastlines with smaller and smaller details are like mathematical objects called fractals. Fractals are infinitely complicated shapes that look similar no matter how much you magnify their details. Some, like the Koch snowflake, look exactly the same however much you zoom in; they're made up of identical copies of themselves. Others, like the Mandelbrot set, look similar as you zoom in but not exactly the same.

Mathematicians first began to dream up shapes such as fractals in the 19th century. But it wasn't until the late 1970s, when computers powerful enough to draw high-resolution graphics became widespread, that anyone saw what a complicated fractal looked like in any detail.

OUCH!

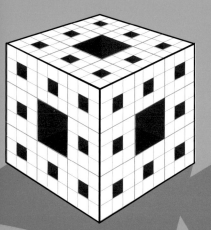

Try this at home

A simple fractal to draw is the Koch snowflake. Draw an equilateral triangle, and divide each side into three. Draw an equilateral triangle in the middle of each side. Erase the base of the smaller triangles to leave a six-pointed star.

Repeat the process, adding 12 more triangles, and repeat again. The area of the snowflake is finite, but the perimeter is infinitely long. At each step, every side grows by $1/3$ of its length—in theory, it could do so forever.

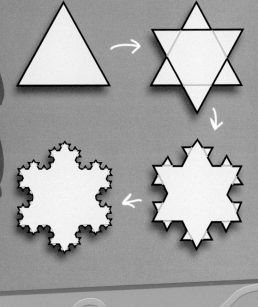

THE IMAGINARY WORLD

Imaginary numbers used in aeronautical design help keep planes up in the air.

Ancient Greek mathematicians believed all numbers were rational until Hippasus showed that wasn't true. The gods are said to have punished Hippasus by drowning him: But he was right.

Mathematicians have been shocked again since then by a new kind of number.

New kinds of numbers always caused problems. No one knows what to make of them. So in the 16th century, when Italian mathematicians started playing around with $\sqrt{-1}$, they said it was just a "fictitious number." Later the Frenchman René Descartes called it "imaginary," and in the 18th century the Swiss Leonard Euler shortened it to i.

Ah ... what a beautiful place!

Rootin' tootin' square root

What exactly is $\sqrt{-1}$ or i? This one single number opens up a whole new way of looking at numbers that takes mathematicians into a strange landscape. The essential problem with $\sqrt{-1}$ is that it can't exist. When you multiply two negative numbers, you always end up with a positive number. So how can -1, a negative number, have a square root?

Iconic number
i for incredible

The imaginary number i really is incredible. It lets us figure out math that would be impossible in the real number system. For example, you can't solve equations that need the square root of a negative number, such as $x^2 = -1$, using real numbers. With i, you can solve it and all others like it.

I told you they existed!!!

Hippasus shocked the other Pythagoreans, who thought that all numbers were rational.

THE JULIA SET
In a Julia set, you can zoom into the pattern as much as you like, and you'll see smaller versions of itself.

The complex plane is home to strange mathematical patterns. They include an infinitely complicated fractal called the Julia set.

The answer is that it can't, at least not on the real number line. But it can have a square root as an imaginary number.

More real than the reals
Despite their "imaginary" part, complex numbers are more real than the real numbers! Our best mathematical models of the universe, which describe how air flows around a wing or electricity flows through cables, for example, all rely on complex numbers.

A beautiful place
Imaginary numbers can be arranged on an imaginary number line. You can arrange the real and imaginary number lines at right angles to create an infinite 2D space called the complex plane. A point in this plane is called a complex number. It has a real part and an imaginary part, like a grid reference.

Dangerous numbers

WANTED!
PUBLIC ENEMY NUMBER 1
Negative, irrational, and imaginary numbers on the loose
Do not approach!
THESE NUMBERS ARE ARMED AND EXTREMELY DANGEROUS

Hippasus is said to have paid with his life for suggesting that irrational numbers existed (even though he was right). And that wasn't the last time that a new idea was seen as wild and dangerous. European mathematicians thought negative numbers were crazy for hundreds of years after the Chinese and Indians had been using them in daily calculations. So when yet another kind of number arrived on the scene, even those who supported it played it safe and called it "imaginary."

ALL OUT OF SHAPE

There's a planet on which wheels are square and soap bubbles are cubes. The roads are just bumps, yet cars roll smoothly. For flat roads, there are special wheels shaped like curved triangles and pentagons.

That planet is closer than you might think. Right here on Earth, it's possible to make precisely square wheels roll perfectly smoothly. But you need a special road. The surface needs to be shaped as a series of curves called catenaries. A catenary is the curve that a chain or rope makes as it hangs under gravity from two supports. In fact, if you have the matching road surface, you can have wheels that are any regular polygon. The real difficulty comes with triangular wheels, which dig into the road surface and mangle it up. You *could* have a vehicle with triangular wheels, but you would have to lay the section of the road just in front of the wheel and it would have to pull the road up behind as it traveled. Not very practical!

Who needs tickets with a view like this!

Try this at home:
Draw a Reuleaux triangle

Draw an equilateral triangle. Place a compass point on one corner of the triangle and use the compass to draw the arc of a circle that touches both corners on the opposite side of the triangle. Move the compass to the next corner and draw another arc on the opposite side. Complete the shape by moving the compass again and drawing the third arc.

Reuleaux polygons

There are an infinite number of shapes called Reuleaux polygons that will roll smoothly on a flat surface. These shapes have curved sides and a constant diameter, which is the width measured through the center. Reuleaux triangles are used in drill bits that drill square holes. If you visit the U.K., you might find a Reuleaux heptagon in your pocket (it's the shape of a 20-pence or 50-pence coin).

Reuleaux triangles are sometimes used for manhole covers.

Soap bubbles

A normal soap bubble is almost a perfect sphere, and a film of soap trapped in a round loop of wire is almost perfectly flat. A soap film tries to make its area as small as possible. This kind of shape is called a minimal surface. If it has a volume of air trapped in it (as in a normal soap bubble), the shape that minimizes the surface area for that volume is a sphere.

Try this at home:
Make a cubic soap bubble

Bend some stiff wire to make a cubic frame with a handle. Dip this into a solution of dish detergent diluted with a little water. See if you can get an (almost) cubic soap bubble in the center of the frame. Soap films can take different shapes in the wire frames, so if you repeat the activity, you should be able to find more shapes.

TESSELLATIONS

How many different wallpaper designs exist?
How many ways can you tile a floor?
What connects these questions, and what
do they have to do with
the decorations in a
14th-century palace?

Periodic tilings

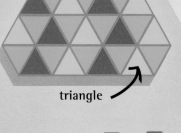

triangle

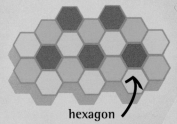

hexagon

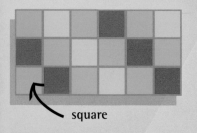

square

Tiles at the
Alhambra Palace

To tessellate, or tile, a plane (flat surface) means to cover it with repeated shapes, without overlaps or gaps. Floor tiles and wallpaper patterns both tessellate a plane. Tessellations have been used for decoration for centuries, especially in Islamic cultures, where religious rules forbid artists from showing the human body. Tiles tessellate due to their shape, but they can also have painted designs that create another layer of pattern.

How many different patterns are there? The key to the question is to look at the different symmetries that occur in tessellations. When you organize by symmetry, then all of the infinitely many possible patterns of wallpaper turn out to be variations of just 17 basic types. In the 14th century, Islamic builders used all 17 patterns of tiles in the Alhambra Palace in Granada, Spain.

Not again.

Periodic tiling with
different polygons

Try this at home

These two "rhombs" can be used together to tile a plane nonperiodically (see explanation, right). Copy and cut out the shapes. Arrange them so that the blue and red curves make continuous shapes (or loops). Can you force the tiling to repeat periodically? Look for "enlargements," as in the sphinx tile, where a group of tiles can be joined to make a larger group of the same shape. This tiling was discovered by Roger Penrose in 1973.

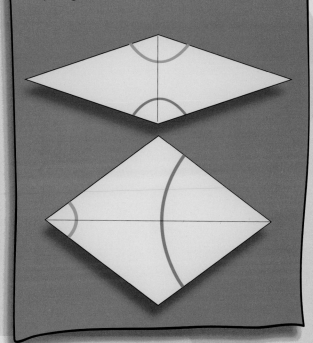

Periodic and nonperiodic tilings

Most tessellations are periodic: You can "pick up" the pattern and shift it so that it fits exactly over itself. Only three tilings are possible using regular polygons: the equilateral triangle, the square, and the hexagon. If you can combine different regular polygons, there are eight more types. With nonregular polygons, there are infinitely many different tilings: Any triangle or quadrilateral will tile a plane.

It's possible to tile any area nonperiodically. This means that there is order to the pattern, but it is not a simple "pick up and shift" repetition. Radial tilings, for example, grow out from a center that has axes of symmetry passing through it.

Some shapes, called rep-tiles, can be arranged to make larger copies of themselves. Four copies of this rep-tile, called the sphinx, make up a bigger sphinx. You can use the sphinx in periodic and nonperiodic tilings.

What kind of sphinx is THAT?

Rep-tiles

I think it's modern art ...

INTO THE 4TH DIMENSION

You must have heard rumors about the fourth dimension. But where is it? You can go everywhere just by moving up or down, left or right, and forward or backward. So where is there room for another direction of motion?

Wow!

We live in a 3-dimensional (3D) universe—at least, as far as everyday life is concerned. To fix a point in space, we need just three numbers. Surfaces are 2D—any point on Earth can be given by just two numbers, latitude and longitude. And along a 1D line, we can tell where we are with one number. So if dimension just means how many numbers it takes to say where you are, then a 4D space is simply one that requires four numbers.

And why stop at four? For mathematicians, even an infinite number of dimensions doesn't pose a problem. And higher dimensions even have practical uses: Codes used to catch errors in digital data are based on the problem of fitting spheres into a 24D space.

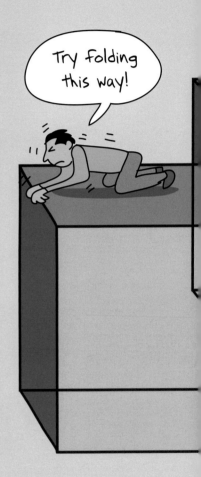

Try folding this way!

RENÉ DESCARTES 1596–1650

Descartes is famous for his philosophy (he's the *"I think, therefore I am"* guy), but he also made advances in math. While lying in bed, he watched a fly moving on the ceiling. Descartes realized that he could fix its position using only two numbers (now called Cartesian coordinates). By describing the shape of the fly's path using numbers and equations, he made a link between geometry and algebra.

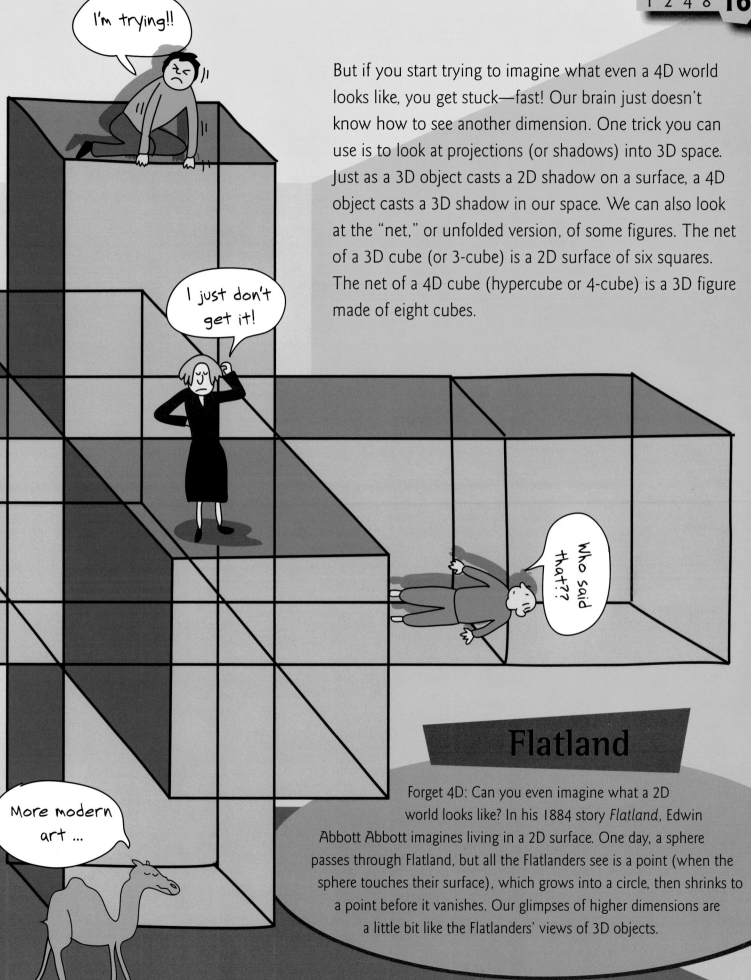

But if you start trying to imagine what even a 4D world looks like, you get stuck—fast! Our brain just doesn't know how to see another dimension. One trick you can use is to look at projections (or shadows) into 3D space. Just as a 3D object casts a 2D shadow on a surface, a 4D object casts a 3D shadow in our space. We can also look at the "net," or unfolded version, of some figures. The net of a 3D cube (or 3-cube) is a 2D surface of six squares. The net of a 4D cube (hypercube or 4-cube) is a 3D figure made of eight cubes.

Flatland

Forget 4D: Can you even imagine what a 2D world looks like? In his 1884 story *Flatland*, Edwin Abbott Abbott imagines living in a 2D surface. One day, a sphere passes through Flatland, but all the Flatlanders see is a point (when the sphere touches their surface), which grows into a circle, then shrinks to a point before it vanishes. Our glimpses of higher dimensions are a little bit like the Flatlanders' views of 3D objects.

IMPOSSIBLE OBJECTS

Math is full of fantastic objects —bottles with no insides (or outsides), one-edged loops, and solid balls with no fixed size. And you can make some of them with just paper and glue!

MÖBIUS STRIP

It's a 2D shape with a twist. It has just one edge, and if you lived on one, you'd never know if you were right-handed or left! If you join two of them together, you get a bottle with no inside—and no outside!

This bizarre-sounding object is a Möbius strip, and it is actually very easy to make. The strip is a mathematical surface, meaning that it doesn't have any thickness (though any real model of one does). If you were living on, or rather in, one, then you'd be visible from either side, as if it were transparent. If you are left-handed, say, and take a tour around the strip once, you return as right-handed!

Try this:
Make a Möbius strip

You'll need some strips of clear acetate or tracing paper about 12 in. x 1¼ in. (30cm x 3cm), some tape or glue, and a pair of scissors.

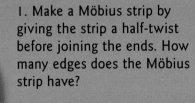

1. Make a Möbius strip by giving the strip a half-twist before joining the ends. How many edges does the Möbius strip have?

2. Now cut along the middle of the Möbius strip. What happens? Look carefully at what you get and count the edges. Cut along the middle again. What happens?

3. Make another Möbius strip, and this time cut it along a line ¹/₃ the way across. What happens this time?

The recycling logo

In 1970, Gary Anderson designed a symbol based on a Möbius strip that has become recognized worldwide as a symbol for recycling. Not all recycling symbols are Möbius strips, like Anderson's original. Look around and try and identify an original version! This one *is* a Möbius strip; You can see how two of the arrows fold over themselves and one folds under.

That's not all of the tricks up Möbius' sleeve, though …. If you take two Möbius strips and glue them edge to edge, you end up with a shape called a Klein bottle. But, this is one trick that you won't be able to do—you would have to move into 4D space to do the gluing, because the surface has to pass through itself without a hole.

The Klein bottle's inside is its outside.

And how am I supposed to get in there??

A PEA THE SIZE OF THE SUN

This solid ball is about the size of a pea. But it has a secret—you can slice it into five different pieces and reassemble them without stretching, to make another ball the size of the Sun!

Clearly, this is nonsense. But such a ball exists! Sort of … Before you get busy in the kitchen, this is a mathematical idea. It's impossible to do it with any real pea or knife. We're talking about a perfect mathematical ball, which is made up of infinitely many points (of course, you'd have to have a perfect knife to go with it). There's a mathematical theorem discovered in 1924, called the Banach–Tarski paradox, that says you can do this and it explains exactly how!

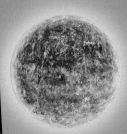

GRAPHS AND NETWORKS

The old Prussian city of Könisberg had seven bridges between the banks and two islands in a river. Was it possible for a walk to cross each bridge only once?

The man who answered the question was the Swiss mathematician Leonhard Euler. In 1736, his solution to the problem laid the foundations for a new branch of mathematics called graph theory.

Graph-ic solution

Euler turned a map of the river and the bridges into a simple diagram (a graph). The graph had vertices (points) representing land, joined by edges (lines) for bridges. Euler showed the walk is only possible if the graph has 0 or 2 vertices where an odd number of edges meet—but this one has 4.

LEONHARD EULER

One of the greatest mathematicians ever, Leonhard Euler (1707–1783) kept working even after going blind in his 50s. Euler's formula $v + f = e + 2$ about the number of vertices (v), faces (f), and edges (e) of a polyhedron is related to graph theory. Euler had an incredible memory and could do huge calculations in his head.

Könisberg

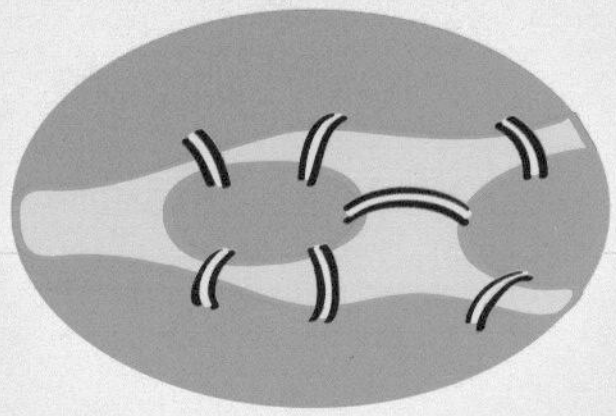

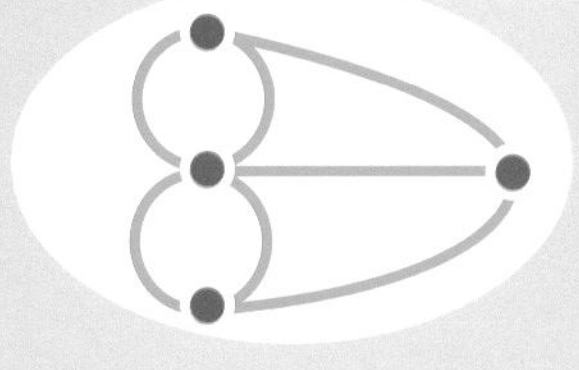

A vertex can be either odd or even (depending on the number of edges that meet there).

Map of bridges in Könisberg

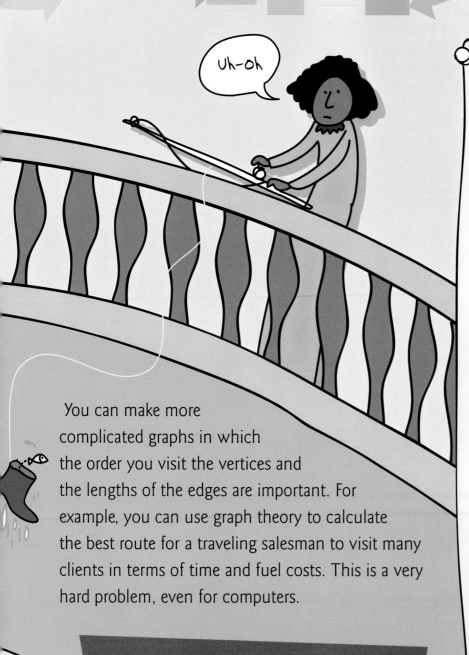

Uh-oh

You can make more complicated graphs in which the order you visit the vertices and the lengths of the edges are important. For example, you can use graph theory to calculate the best route for a traveling salesman to visit many clients in terms of time and fuel costs. This is a very hard problem, even for computers.

Six degrees of separation

Graph theory can be applied to human relationships. It shows that, on average, you're only six steps away from any other person: that is, you know someone who knows someone who knows someone … and so on, six times. You're two steps away from friends of friends, but you might be many more steps from someone in the forests of New Guinea. Social networking sites use graphs to measure how members are connected to each other.

Try this at home:
The utilities problem

Suppose three houses each need a single connection to the gas, water, and electricity companies. Can you do it without any of the connections crossing? (You're not allowed to pass a connection through a utility company or a house).

NOW TRY IT ON A TORUS
First, find yourself a torus—that's a shape like a doughnut with a hole. An inflatable ring or a bagel will do (doughnuts are too sticky). Now mark three houses and three utility companies on the surface of the torus, and see if it's easier to solve the problem.

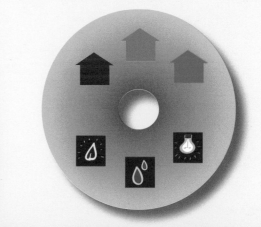

THE LIVING WORLD

What do math and biology have to do with each other? Not much, at first sight. But people have observed symmetry in living things since ancient times, and by the 19th century, mathematicians had developed models to describe how populations increase and how new leaves grow on plants.

It wasn't until the 20th century, though, that mathematical biology exploded to become one of the hottest areas of research. Three main developments made this possible: chaos theory in math, the discovery of DNA in biology, and the growth of computer power. Chaos theory helped mathematicians and biologists understand why, for example, population sizes change in unpredictable ways. The discovery of DNA and gene theory meant that lots of areas of math, from codes to knot theory, could be used to investigate living things. And powerful computers have made it possible to create complex models of all kinds of things, from cells to swarms to ecosystems.

Ahh ... nice and symmetrical!

THE RIGHT SIZE

Why can't a cat be as big as a horse? How do ants lift 100 times their own weight, while humans struggle to lift our own? Why can a mouse survive a fall that would kill an elephant?

The key to such questions is the idea of scaling, or making things bigger or smaller. It's not entirely straightforward. The volume (and therefore, the mass, or amount of tissue) in an animal increases as a cube, while other features such as strength increase by a square law.

Take a gazelle. Gazelles have very thin legs. If gazelles were twice as large in every dimension, their weight would increase by a cube law (8 times). But the thickness (area) of their bones would only increase by a square law (4 times). The same amount of bone would have to support twice as much weight—and would be in danger of snapping!

Scaling is also the reason ants can carry many times their own weight, while larger animals struggle with proportionally much smaller loads. Body weight increases with the cube of height, but muscle strength, which depends on the thickness (area) of muscle fibers, increases only as the square. So larger creatures struggle with proportionally much less.

PUT ME DOWN!

Raining ants and elephants

How can an ant or a mouse survive a fall that would kill an elephant (or even a human)? When an object falls, Earth's gravity makes it accelerate. The faster it travels, the stronger the force of air resistance it meets. Eventually, the push of air resistance and the pull of gravity balance, and the object stops accelerating. It reaches top speed, or terminal velocity.

The force due to gravity (or weight) grows with mass, as the cube of an animal's length. But air resistance grows with surface area, or the square of the length. This means that bigger animals have much higher terminal velocities, and so are less likely to survive a fall because higher terminal velocity means a bigger impact. Ouch!

Even I can't survive THIS fall!

SCALING

When you double the side of a square, its area doesn't just double: It becomes $2^2 = 4$ times as big. When you double the side of a cube, its surface area becomes 4 times as big (called a square law), and its volume becomes $2^3 = 8$ times as big (a cube law).

Sides twice as long make an area 4 times as big.

Once times its mass is heavy enough!

Doubling the sides of a cube makes its volume—and mass— 8 times as big.

LIKE RABBITS

What do rabbits, pineapples, and an irrational ratio have in common? Only the most famous number sequence in math: the Fibonacci sequence.

The Fibonacci sequence is named after the Italian mathematician who introduced it to Europe. In his book on arithmetic, *Liber Abaci*, Fibonacci asks a simple question about breeding rabbits.

A rabbit problem

"Suppose baby rabbits take a month to grow into adults. Then they mate every month, and a month later, a pair of babies (one male, one female) is born. As each baby pair becomes adult, it produces its own babies, and none of the rabbits die. If you start with one male–female pair of baby rabbits in January, how many pairs of rabbits will you have at the end of the year?"

Fibonacci showed that, at the end of the first and second months, there would still be one pair, But in the months that followed, there would be 2, 3, 5, 8, 13, 21, 34 … pairs, growing to 144 pairs by the 12th month. The sequence could go on forever.

The Fibonacci sequence …

1, 1, 2, 3, 5, 8, 13, 21, 34, 55, 89, 144, 233, 377, 610, 987, 1597, 2584, 4181, 6765, 10946, 17711, 28657, 46368, 75025, 121393, 196418, ...

… 21, 34, 55, 89 …

FIBONACCI

Leonardo Fibonacci (c.1170–1250) studied mathematics in North Africa. From Arab mathematicians there, he learned about the Indian decimal system. In his book *Liber Abaci*, Fibonacci introduced the decimal system to Europe. He showed how it was much better for arithmetic than Roman numerals. Fibonacci wrote several other important books on geometry and algebra.

PAIRS OF RABBITS

Fibonacci's simple question about pairs of rabbits produces a sequence that can grow without limit. The pattern has been found throughout the natural world. It occurs in the number of branches on a tree, the number of florets in a cauliflower, petals in a daisy, or in the bumps of a pineapple.

1

1

2

3

5

8

We can write an easy equation to find Fibonacci numbers if we call the first number F_1, the second F_2, the third F_3, and so on. Every Fibonacci number from F_3 on is the sum of the previous two numbers:

$F_3 = F_2 + F_1$ $(2 = 1 + 1)$

$F_4 = F_3 + F_2$ $(3 = 2 + 1)$

$F_5 = F_4 + F_3$ $(5 = 3 + 2)$

Real rabbits don't breed like this—or the universe would be full of rabbits. But the Fibonacci numbers do turn up all over the place in nature, and they have fascinated mathematicians for centuries. One of the most interesting properties is the ratio of successive Fibonacci numbers. Farther along the sequence, the ratio between successive numbers (the larger number divided by the smaller) gets closer and closer to an irrational number called the golden ratio, or Φ (phi).

The sequence occurs in the spiraling florets of a cauliflower.

Iconic number

Φ (phi), the golden ratio

$$\Phi = \frac{1 + \sqrt{5}}{2} \approx 1.618$$

(≈ means approximately equals.)
The golden ratio is the ratio between two parts of a line segment that is divided such

that the ratio of the entire segment (a + b) to the larger part (a) is the same as the ratio of the larger part (a) to the smaller part (b). The golden ratio gets its name because people find it beautiful. It has turned up in paintings and buildings since ancient times.

AB/AC = AC/CB = 1.618

A   C   B

ANIMAL POPULATIONS

Why do some species flourish while others die out? Math can help biologists model how populations change in an ecosystem.

A population model is a mathematical formula that predicts how a population will change. The simplest models are based on exponential growth, In these models, the bigger the population, the faster it grows. But in the real world, population growth is limited by factors such as how much food is available. Different models can help predict what happens when several species compete for food … or hunt one another for food.

The equations used in these models look simple, but the predictions they make are not. In some cases, a population stabilizes; in others, it's periodic, growing and shrinking repeatedly. And sometimes, there's complete chaos!

EXPONENTIAL GROWTH
In exponential growth, a population grows more quickly the bigger it is. Its growth curve soon becomes very steep. In real life, however, exponential population growth only continues for short periods before outside factors interrupt it.

Population

Time

PREDATORS AND PREY

Suppose one species hunts another, such as wolves and moose. When there are too many wolves, their population falls because there is a food shortage. This allows the moose population to rise again, which leads to more wolves, so the cycle continues. Reality is more complicated: For example, disease or changes in climate could affect the moose's own food supply.

Wolf population increases

Moose population falls

Moose population increases

Wolf population falls

MATHEMATICAL CHAOS

You might think that chaos just means utter confusion. But in math, *chaos* means something very precise: "sensitive dependence on initial conditions." In other words, say you have two identical ecosystems with slightly different starting populations of wolves and moose. Some years later, their populations might be very different. (Perhaps in one, both wolves and moose die out, while in the other, wolves and moose remain in a periodic relationship.) This mathematical chaos happens even in very simple population models: It has nothing to do with how complicated the real world actually is.

It's chaos!

CENSUS

We're not a-moosed ...

Bacteria, bacteria everywhere

A bacterial cell reproduces by splitting in two. Each new cell splits into two, so the population doubles each generation. This exponential growth is *explosively* fast. Start with a single bacterium (a thousand-millionth of a gram!) that reproduces every 10 minutes. After 10 minutes, you'd have 2 bacteria; after 20, 4, and after an hour, 64. That may not sound like much, but in less than a day, the colony would outweigh Earth!

So why haven't bacteria taken over the universe? Well, the rate of growth can't continue exponentially because the bacteria run out of food. Although many populations start growing exponentially, none grow like it for very long.

The number you are calling is irrational!

Iconic number

e, EULER'S NUMBER

$e = 2.71828 \ldots$ is an irrational number like π. It crops up all over mathematics, including whenever something grows exponentially. As long as growth is proportional to a population, you'll find e somewhere. In the 17th century, Jacob Bernoulli found e when he was studying how money grows because of bank interest. Leonhard Euler later found a formula for it: $e = 1 + {}^1/_{1!} + {}^1/_{2!} + {}^1/_{3!} + \ldots$

If you want to get an idea of scale and complexity, you don't need to look farther than your own body. You'll even find symmetries and fractals.

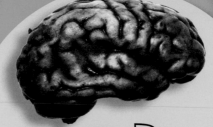

3.3
The weight of an adult brain in pounds (1.5kg); although it makes up only 2 percent of the mass of the whole body, it uses 20 percent of the body's energy.

2
The length in yards (meters) of tightly coiled DNA in each of your cells (except red blood cells).

2.4
The area in square yards (2m²) covered by an adult's skin, the largest organ.

YOUR BODY IN NUMBERS

Try this at home

Although humans are symmetrical, the symmetry isn't perfect. Put a mirror down the middle of a photo to see what you'd look like if both sides of your face were exactly the same. We're not symmetrical inside, of course—and most of us also have a strong handedness (left or right).

Not quite ...

Like many animals, humans are bilaterally symmetric. This means that there is a single plane (slice) through the middle of the body that divides it into mirror images.

Fractals in the body

Blood vessels branch out from the major arteries and veins into smaller vessels and finally into capillaries, just like the branching of a river or a tree. The network of blood vessels is a natural fractal—it looks pretty much the same when you zoom into it. This is also true of airways in the lungs.

Fractals turn up in other ways in the body. Although a heartbeat is approximately regular, its rhythm has fractal patterns in it.

3 BILLION
The number of times your heart will beat if you live to be 80!

224
The maximum speed, in miles per hour (360km/h), at which nerve cells carry electrical signals. Signals that tell you where your muscles are travel very fast; pain signals are usually slower.

100,000
The approximate number of hairs on your head (if you're not going bald!).

2,000,000
The number of new red blood cells your body makes every second—to replace the 2 million that die in that time!

206
The number of bones in your skeleton—¼ of which are in your feet! The smallest is in your ear and is less than 0.1 in. (3mm) long; the longest, your femur or thigh bone, is nearly ¼ of your height.

6
The number of months it takes your nails to grow from the base to the tip.

4
The number of different "nucleotide bases" in the sequence contained in human DNA; the sequence is about 3 billion bases long.

LESS THAN 1
The number of minutes it takes for a red blood cell to go all around your body.

The lungs pack a huge area into a small volume. Just as the Koch snowflake has an infinite perimeter within a finite area, so your lungs pack an area of 84 square yards (70 m²), or about half a tennis court, into your chest!

How many yous are you?
You're just one individual, right? Well, not quite. It's true that, although you have about 100 trillion cells all together, they form only one organism. But your skin is covered in bacteria—millions per square inch, even after you've washed your hands—and there are hundreds of different types living in your gut, many of which are essential to digestion. In all, there are 10 times more bacteria, fungi, and other organisms living on or in you than your own cells (but since they're much smaller, they make up only about 1 percent of your mass).

5
The age in days of the oldest cells in your gut. The cells of the cortex in the brain are as old as you are.

99
The percentage of your DNA you share with all other humans; You share over 95 percent with chimpanzees, our closest relatives.

WHAT IS LIFE?

It's not just biologists who think about life. Some scientists believe that computers can display all the important features of life. And just as computers can mimic life, so the stuff that shapes biological life, DNA, can work as a computer!

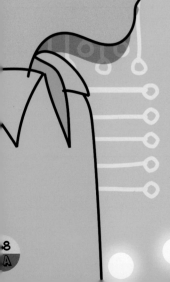

And what kind of food do you like?

Oh! Only natural and organic ... I can't STAND artificial stuff!

Humans have been fascinated by the idea of intelligent and living machines for hundreds of years. By the mid-20th century, mathematicians had developed the basic ideas of artificial intelligence and artificial life. Together with philosophers and computer scientists, they now use these ideas to investigate what being "conscious" means, how animals behave, and how life began.

What would a living computer be like? We'd want it to be intelligent—to be able to think, in other words—and it would have to be able to reproduce. British mathematician Alan Turing invented a test called the Turing test. The test poses some questions. If a machine's answers can't be told apart from a human's, then the machine is said to be "intelligent"—well, at least as far as the test is concerned.

Try this at home:
Life—but not as we know it

"Life," invented by John Conway in 1970, is a "self-playing" game. It has a grid of cells, which can be either dead or alive. Each cell has eight neighbors and lives or dies according to simple rules (below). Play begins by choosing a starting pattern of live cells. Then the rules determine what happens next to each cell in a series of regular moves. What makes "Life" so fascinating for biologists, computer scientists, and philosophers is that its simple rules and initial patterns produce complex behavior that looks like (biological) life. Some patterns stay fixed, others oscillate, and others create or gobble up other patterns. To see how "Life" works, try an online or downloadable computer version such as Golly.

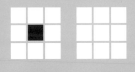

1. A live cell with fewer than two live neighbors dies (loneliness).

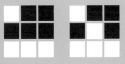

2. A live cell with more than three live neighbors dies (overcrowding).

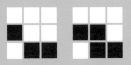

3. A dead cell with exactly three live neighbors becomes alive.

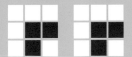

4. A live cell with two or three live neighbors remains alive.

Hello!

Nice to meet you!

DNA computing

DNA molecules, which are found in most cells of all living organisms, carry "instructions for life." DNA determines what you look like and how to build and repair your body, just as a computer stores both data and programs.

Turing showed that any computer program could be broken down into extremely simple instructions, such as "copy these symbols." And copying symbols is effectively what happens as the DNA molecule works. So it's possible to make a computer that uses DNA to calculate. The inputs and outputs to a DNA computer are molecules, rather than electrical signals. DNA computers have been designed that can calculate square roots and even make patterns known as fractals.

ARTIFICIAL LIFE

A-life, or artificial life, models are related to programs like Conway's "Life." In 1986, Craig Reynolds made an A-life model as a computer graphics program called Boids. Boids makes a set of points in space move as if they were birds in a flock. According to the rules, points (boids) stay close together and move in the same direction as the whole set (the flock). If you put an obstruction in the path of the boids, the flock divides as it approaches it and then regroups on the other side—just like a real flock of birds!

EVERYDAY LIFE

Patterns surround us in everyday life, and wherever there's a pattern, there's math. There are natural or learned patterns in things that we all do unconsciously: sorting a deck of cards, tying shoelaces, and even using language (if you're writing in English, there's a good chance that you've written more "e"s than any other letter).

In some cases, someone has deliberately designed a pattern, but we don't really notice it. That's true about the way that tournament playoffs are arranged, for example, or the order in which people board a plane. These patterns are of different types, for example, of the order of events or of instructions or of shapes. And some patterns, such as those in tossing a coin or rolling a die, only emerge when you take a long view and observe an event repeated many times. But math doesn't just help reveal patterns and information: It can also help hide them. Phone calls, bank account information, and online identity are kept private using secret codes that rely on large prime numbers.

Math is often used to make models (descriptions) of the real world, such as voting patterns, the flight of a ball, or the inside of a star. When the models are good, they can be used to predict and understand our universe. But a lot of math doesn't seem to have to do with anything other than ideas (patterns in the mind— such as 4-dimensional cubes, for example).

Hmmm ...
E-e-E-e-E-e-E

Please enter 7-digit password
- - - - - - -

CHOICES, CHOICES

Yummy!

Two scoops from three flavors gives six possible permutations

If there are three flavors—strawberry, chocolate, and vanilla —and you're only allowed one scoop, then your life is easy. Relatively. But what if you go for two scoops of different flavors? Then you have three choices for the first scoop but only two choices for the second. If you choose strawberry for the first scoop, then you can only choose chocolate or vanilla for the second. So for each of three choices for the first scoop, you have two further choices for the second: six possible choices in total. (That's counting strawberry on top of chocolate as a different choice from chocolate on top of strawberry.) This kind of choice, where the order of the scoops matters, is called a permutation.

$7 \times 7 \times 3$
$\times 7 \times 5 \ldots$

Repeating flavors

If you're allowed to repeat flavors, then calculating permutations is easy. Say you're hungry enough for three scoops, and there are seven flavors. Then you have seven choices for the first scoop. For each of these, you have a further seven choices for the second scoop. And for each of these choices, you have a further seven choices for the third scoop. So in total, you have $7 \times 7 \times 7 = 7^3 = 343$ choices.

"COMBINATION" LOCK

When you're unlocking a combination lock, the order of the digits matters. If the unlocking code is 1689, say, putting in the same digits in another order —1968—won't work. So, really these locks ought to be called "permutation locks!"

This might help ...

If you're allowed three scoops, and there's a choice of 35 flavors, then there are $35 \times 34 \times 33 = 39{,}270$ permutations. That should be enough for a different permutation for every day of your life!

Combinations

If you're not fussy about the order of flavors, so that you count strawberry on top of chocolate as the same as chocolate on strawberry, then the number of choices is smaller. A choice where order doesn't matter is called a combination. If you have three flavors and don't use any more than once, there are only three possible combinations of a two-scoop cone.

I have the ace of spades.

Doh! What's a spade??

PICK A CARD, ANY CARD

A deck of playing cards has 52 different cards. How many ways can the deck be arranged? (Order matters, so we're figuring out a permutation.)

There are 52 possible choices for the first card, 51 for the second, 50 for the third, and so on. The total number of arrangements is $52 \times 51 \times 50 \times \cdots \times 3 \times 2 \times 1 = 52!$ (! is the symbol for factorial). The result is a number with 68 digits. If everyone who is alive today each rearranged a billion decks of cards into new permutations a billion times each second, they'd have to keep going for more than a thousand billion billion billion centuries to cover all the possibilities: That's much longer than the universe has existed!

How many different hands of seven cards are there? That's a much smaller number, which equals $52 \times 51 \times 50 \times 49 \times 48 \times 47 \times 46$. It still comes to more than 600 billion.

CHANCE AND RISK

Ooh ... risky!

We live in an uncertain world. We can't predict the weather exactly or guarantee a lottery win. But the theory of probability can help us predict what will happen in the long run.

A die roll or a coin toss is random (unpredictable), and it wasn't until the 17th century that people began to study sequences of random events. They discovered that, even though any particular random event was unpredictable, if you looked at many rolls or tosses, you would see a pattern. As well as investigating games, mathematicians calculated the probability (risk or chance) of ships carrying precious cargo being lost at sea. This was the beginning of probability theory.

Today, probability theory is important for the business world, for example, in insurance; and also in card games and lotteries. It is also vital in courts, for showing how likely a person is to be guilty, based on the evidence, and in hospitals, where it is used for understanding medical test results.

HEADS, I WIN

Each toss of a coin is independent, which means it doesn't affect any other toss. Throwing a head doesn't make it anymore likely that you'll get a tail next. For a fair coin, the chance of getting a head on any toss is ½ (or 50 percent). You could throw 100 heads in a row. The chances of that happening are exactly the same as throwing 50 heads and 50 tails alternately (H T H T ...) or as any other pattern of 100 tosses.

Don't lose your head!

Figuring out probabilities

You can calculate probabilities by understanding how an event "works." Each score of a fair die is equally likely, because of the way it is made. So the probability of getting a 5, say, on any particular throw is $\frac{1}{6}$. But in order to estimate the risk of a ship being lost at sea, you'd need to look at actual records of how many ships are lost at sea each year.

If something is impossible (such as throwing a 7 with one die), the probability is 0. If something is certain, then the probability is 1, or 100 percent.

Sports stores have to think about the risk of the winter being warm or a summer being cold. Either event could leave them with a lot of unsold skis or surfboards on the shelf. Large sports stores buy insurance against weather that would be bad for business.

I'm just here for the cake.

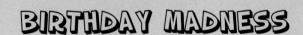

BIRTHDAY MADNESS

What's the chance that two people in your class have the same birthday? Close to impossible? Wrong! If you have more than 23 people in your class, it's more likely than not!

Okay, let's assume that people's birthdays are spread out evenly through the year and independent, meaning that no one's birthday affected the date that anyone else was born. Forgetting complications such as leap years and twins, the chances of you and one friend having different birthdays is $\frac{365}{365} \times \frac{364}{365}$. Your birthday can be on any one of 365 days, and your friend's can be on any of the other 364 days. (When you want the probability of two independent events happening, you multiply them.) In a group of three, the chances of everyone's birthdays being different is $\frac{365}{365} \times \frac{364}{365} \times \frac{363}{365}$, which is about 99 percent. In a group of 10 people, it's about 88 percent. But with 23 people, it's just less than 50 percent: which means the chance of two people sharing a birthday is just over 50 percent.

SAMPLES AND AVERAGES

When was the last time a bunch of mathematicians started poking around in your brain to see what makes you tick? What do you mean, never? When did you last visit a supermarket?

Statistics is all about gathering and interpreting data. When you hear that the average family has 2.1 children or that 67 percent of cats prefer eating birds to mice, you're dealing with statistical estimates. Unlike other areas of mathematics, statistics does not give absolute answers—but it does allow you to make estimates and predictions, and say how inaccurate they might be.

> Hmmm ... I only need 2.7 carrots ...

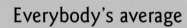

Everybody's average

A key idea in statistics is averages: calculating standard data from a range of samples. Averages are estimations, but they can make data much easier to process. There are three different kinds.

Mean: The simplest kind of average works by adding the data from all the samples and dividing it by the number of the samples.

Median: This type of average sets out the data from the samples in order and takes the middle figure in the list as the average.

Mode: In this type of average, the mode is the value that occurs most times in the list (it's easier to find if the data are in order).

Predictions

Statistics is often used to make predictions about a population of people or things based on data about a sample (a small group from the population). For example, if you picked 10 candies at random from a bag of 100 and 5 were red, you would be able to estimate that half the candies in the bag were red.

This is likely to be more accurate than if you just guessed, and it is much quicker than counting all the candy.

That's super!

Some of the biggest users of statistics are supermarkets. They gather all kinds of data, such as which brands sell best on rainy days or which foods are bought together. They try to use patterns in the data to make more money. For example, they might see that shoppers who buy cheese often buy mustard, so they might create a "bundle deal" to tempt other shoppers to buy both products.

Fat trap

The supermarket has loads of math in action, from the size of cans to prices to the nutritional data about food. But sometimes the numbers can be a little misleading—especially if someone is trying to sell you something. A pack of "healthier" potato chips that are "33 percent reduced fat," for example, might have only 20g of fat instead of 30g—but that doesn't make them low fat. And a cake labeled as "90 percent fat-free" sounds better for you than one that's "10 percent fat."

Wait ... what do you mean they're NOT really low-fat ...

ALGORITHMS

Sort out THIS mess!

You may not have heard of algorithms—but you use them every day. They're how computers sort and find data. An algorithm is a precise, step-by-step method for performing a task, such as sorting or searching.

Computer systems store data in organized collections, or databases. Algorithms are vital for sorting and searching these databases. The computer uses a sorting algorithm to arrange its data, say, from the largest to the smallest. A searching algorithm then helps you find the web site, song, or book you want.

Two ways of sorting

It's a bit difficult to show computer algorithms, so let's use playing cards. Suppose you want to sort a deck of cards from the lowest to the highest. Here are two algorithms that you could use:

Insertion sort: You'd probably use this algorithm automatically. Use the first card to start a new pile. Take the second card and put it in the correct place in the new pile (before or after the first). Repeat for the third card, fourth card, etc. When you reach the last card, your new pile will be sorted.

BAKING   ECONOMICS   FRENCH   GARDENING   HERBS   INTERNET   JOKES   KAYAKING   LIMERICKS

The bubble sort: Compare cards 1 and 2. If card 2 is lower than card 1, swap them. Now compare cards 2 and 3: swap if necessary. Continue to the end of the pack, then start again. When you can go through the pack with no swaps, it's sorted. (This is called a "bubble sort" because lower cards "bubble" to the front.)

A binary search only works if the cards are sorted.

Two types of searches

Now let's search for a particular card. In an unsorted deck, you could just check each card. Your card might be the first one, but it could be the 52nd! This is a linear or sequential search.

If the deck is sorted, however, you can use a binary search. Divide the deck in half and check if your card is higher than the last card in the lower half of the deck. If it is, ignore the lower half; halve the higher half and repeat the process. After one step, you'll have 26 cards left; after the second, 13 … by the sixth step, you'll have found the card!

Escape from a maze

If you're stuck in a maze, two algorithms could help you get out. The first is the "random mouse." At every junction you choose a direction at random. You might get out— but you might end up going around forever. The "wall following" algorithm is a surefire way to solve a simple maze. You keep one hand in contact with a wall as you walk. Eventually, it will bring you out.

AL-KHWARIZMI
(C. A.D. 780–850)

Al-Khwarizmi was an Islamic mathematician at the House of Wisdom in Baghdad. Al-Khwarizmi introduced the Indian decimal number system to the West, and like many mathematicians of the times, he was also an astronomer. The word *algebra* comes from one of his methods for solving equations. Both the words *algorism*—the method for doing arithmetic with the decimal system—and *algorithm* were named after him.

That's a-maze-ing!

KEEPING SECRETS

Whenever there's something to win or lose, from a war to a business deal, there are secrets. And where there are secrets, there are people making codes and codebreakers trying to crack them.

Shhhh!

The Enigma machine coded German messages in World War II.

In the oldest kind of cipher (secret code), each letter of the message you want to keep secret (the "plaintext") is replaced by a different letter to create the "ciphertext." For example, you could replace each letter in a word by the previous letter in the alphabet (the letter "a" is replaced by "z"). In this case, the word "bee" becomes "add." The rule is the "key" to the cipher, which the recipient of the message needs to know. But although this kind of cipher was used for many centuries, actually, it's easy to crack. Letters occur with different frequencies in different languages (in English, "e" is the most common, followed by "t" and "a"). If the most frequent letter in the ciphertext is "j," for example, then it's likely that the "j" stands for "e."

CIPHER KEY

You use a cipher key by substituting the letter in the top row (plaintext) with the letter beneath it (ciphertext).

A B C D E F G H I J K L M N O P Q R S T U
B C D E F G H I J K L M N O P Q R S T U

Try this at home:
Crack the code

Here's a cipher for you to try to crack. It might help to know that "the" is the most common three-letter word in English. Another clue: How many letters of the alphabet appear in the ciphertext?

Gsv jfrxp yildm ulc qfnkh levi gsv ozab wlt.

Polyalphabetic ciphers

More secure ciphers use different letters to encode each plaintext letter. You can make such a polyalphabetic cipher by drawing a triangular table with the plaintext down one side. Fill in each row with consecutive letters, adding one more letter in each row that follows, and read the ciphertext along the diagonal. Here, TRIANGULAR becomes TSKDRLASIA. In World War II, the German Enigma code used polyalphabetic ciphers that took many mathematicians to crack. They invented one of the first computers to help them!

```
T
R S
I J K
A B C D
N O P Q R
G H I J K L
U V W X Y Z A
L M N O P Q R S
A B C D E F G H I
R S T U V W X Y Z A
```

Public key cryptography

Today, codes are vital to secure communication online. Modern codes use a lot of math and some strange ideas. Public key encryption gets around the problem of how to tell a recipient what the key is by having two keys: one, which everyone knows, to lock the message, and another, which only the recipient knows, to unlock it. You use the recipient's public key to lock a message—and they use their private key to unlock it. In one version, the public key is made by multiplying two large primes together to make a very large (200-digit) number. To crack the private key, you'd have to factorize this number. For even the fastest supercomputers, this would take months … or years!

I've forgotten the key to my code.

Yes. I have to factorize 4,951,755,139,626, 284,227,693,117,441!!

Don't you have a hint?

W X Y Z

W X Y Z A

W X Y Z A

UP IN THE AIR

It's no surprise that there's math behind air transportation. But it's not just about navigation or wing design—math is used to plan networks and price tickets, and even in the way in which you board an aircraft.

Hey! Where's my seat belt?

$0

Anyone for ping-pong?

The next time you fly somewhere, you could ask your neighbor how much their ticket cost. Air fares are famous for varying widely, so they might have paid two or three times as much as you did! On a bus or train journey, in contrast, nearly everyone pays the same. Airlines used to charge in the same way as bus companies: Every seat on a 100-seat plane would be priced at the cost needed to make a profit, say $100.

Today, airlines use a more complicated pricing policy. They might offer 90 seats at an "early bird" price of $90 for people who book ahead. The remaining 10 seats cost $200, because there are always a few business travelers who will pay that much but who will not be able to book ahead of time. If the plane is full,

Airline networks

There are two basic ways of linking cities: hub and spoke and point-to-point. Both have their advantages, and airlines use both kinds of networks.

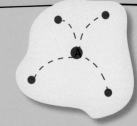

Hub and spoke. The hub city (A) is joined directly to each of the other cities (spokes), but problems at A can jam the whole network.

Point-to-point. Each city is linked to every other city, but there are far more routes to manage.

$150

the airline will still make a profit, even though 90 of the seats are sold at a loss.

In reality, pricing airline tickets requires complicated math to take into account many variables that affect how much customers will pay, such as the time of the flight, the dates of school vacations, or competing offers. Airlines (and hotels, who also use pricing models) use powerful computers to set prices that maximize their profits.

20	40				30	10	50
							49
19	39				29	9	
							48
18	38				28	8	
							47
17	37				27	7	
							46
16	36				26	6	
55						45	
15	35				25	5	
54						44	
14	34				24	4	
53						43	
13	33				23	3	
52						42	
12	32				22	2	
51						41	
11	31				21	1	

One algorithm boards people in alternate row order, filling window seats first. This gives passengers time to settle. (But even random boarding is faster than the traditional method of back to front.)

Scramble for your seats

What's the best way to board a plane? Well, the worst way is to work from front to back: Passengers in the front rows hold everyone else up as they stow their hand luggage. Airlines traditionally board from the last rows forward. But now mathematicians have come up with boarding algorithms that are much faster than this traditional way.

I'd pay more if they moved quicker!

$200

$165

$430

$165

$25

CONSTRUCTION TIME

Architects have a tough job. They have to design buildings that can stand up to high winds and earthquakes but also look attractive. Math lies behind both the engineering and the beauty of buildings.

The main loads that skyscrapers have to support are not the people and equipment inside them, but the force of the wind. Very tall skyscrapers have surfaces designed to deflect the force of the wind, but even so, the top stories sway a yard or two during a storm. Earthquakes can have similar effects. The motion can cause damage and make people inside feel a little worried—or even a little seasick.

Some buildings have a massive "tuned damper" inside to prevent this movement. It is usually a steel or concrete block, hanging on a pendulum or resting on springs. It helps "tune" the building so that it doesn't vibrate so much.

Geodesic domes

Geodesic domes are a little bit like buildings made with a ruler and paper. A geodesic is a curve that is the shortest distance between two points on a sphere (the equivalent of a straight line on a plane). Geodesic domes are spheres (or parts of spheres) made up of a framework of approximate geodesics, which intersect to make triangles. The framework is covered with a skin. Weight for weight, geodesic domes are much stronger than other types of buildings. They do have disadvantages, however. There are lots of joints and edges that must be sealed. And all the walls are curved—you won't be able to hang a painting or put up a shelf!

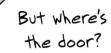

But where's the door?

Arches in Gaudi's Sagrada Família cathedral in Barcelona, Spain

BUILDING UPSIDE DOWN

Spanish architect Antoni Gaudí (1852-1926) is known for his beautifully curved buildings. The curves he used are precise mathematical shapes called catenaries. A chain hanging under its own weight makes the shape of a catenary, and an upside-down catenary makes a perfect arch. The only force acting on a hanging chain is tension, or pulling force. When you turn the shape upside down, the only force is a compressive, or pushing one—the kind of force that an arch supports best. Gaudi designed his structures upside down by hanging different chains from a surface to represent arches.

Tuned damper

All objects have a natural frequency. This is the rate at which they vibrate or move if given a push or pull. A guitar string vibrates at its natural frequency when plucked, for example, and a swing or pendulum swings with its natural frequency. If you push an object at a frequency close to its natural frequency, it makes bigger movements.

Buildings also have natural frequencies, which means they can be "tuned" (like violin strings!) so that the wind or tremors don't make them vibrate dangerously.

MATH TALES

Mathematics is like a language, and mathematicians have to translate between their ideas and symbols, and languages such as English, all the time. And math has inspired writers in surprising ways.

What page was I on??

One book that is full of hidden math is *Alice's Adventures in Wonderland* (and the other Alice books). Lewis Carroll, who wrote them in the 1860s and 1870s, was a math professor at the University of Oxford in England. A lot of the "nonsense" in the book has math behind it. Tweedledum and Tweedledee argue with some crafty logic. The Mock Turtle remembers studying "the different branches of Arithmetic—Ambition, Distraction, Uglification, and Derision" (addition, subtraction, multiplication, and division).

The longest poem in the world?

Other authors use math in the structure of their writing. In 1961, French writer Raymond Queneau published "One hundred thousand billion sonnets." Queneau was part of a group of writers called OuLiPo, who were inspired by math. A sonnet is a 14-line poem, but Queneau gave 10 versions of each line (the versions all rhyme). Think of the poem as a 10-page book, with cuts through the pages between the lines.

There are 10 choices for the first line, 10^2 combinations of first and second lines, 10^3 combinations of the first three lines ... and 10^{14} or one hundred thousand billion different 14-line poems in this book. If you read one of the poems every minute, it would take you nearly 200 million years to read all of them!

Little monkeys

You might have heard the theory that if you gave a monkey a typewriter and it hit a key every second, eventually it would type the complete works of Shakespeare ... Well, if you were given an infinite amount of time, this would happen. But it's very unlikely to happen in the lifetime of the universe. (Of course, you could speed always up the process if you had an infinite number of monkeys ...)

AN INFINITE LIBRARY

The Argentinian author Jorge Luis Borges once wrote a story about a library in which there existed every book that could possibly be written (every possible permutation of the letters of the alphabet, spaces, and punctuation marks). Although virtually all of the books would be nonsense, the library would also contain an infinite number of versions of every book with different spelling mistakes and other errors.

Mathematics and music

Explore a piece of music and you'll find ratios, equations, and symmetries. Both math and music are based on abstract patterns. People who like math are often very musical, and vice versa.

The Pythagoreans, for example, were crazy about music as well as mathematics. They defined musical scales using simple ratios. There are other kinds of scales. Some, like the tuning of a normal piano, are based on irrational numbers.

Symmetry occurs throughout music. There is a canon by J. S. Bach whose notation reads the same upside down and back to front.

If there are 60 keys on a keyboard and a monkey types once per second, then 24 monkeys might average one "hello" in a year. A thousand monkeys should manage a "hello world" in a billion years.

A SPORTING CHANCE

Too springy!!!

You cannot be serious! That ball was IN!

Math is essential in sports, and not just for measuring or timing. It also helps organize tournaments and develop equipment and training routines.

Sensors can capture data about athletes in the lab or on the court, recording precise body movements or general patterns of play. These data can be fed into mathematical models that help athletes become more efficient, helping runners adjust their stride, for example, or figuring out how to get power from a golf swing.

Data can also be analyzed using statistical methods to give a picture of a player or a team over a game or over a whole season.

Round robins and eliminations

How do you organize a fair tournament of many competitors? In an elimination tournament, teams or players are paired up and the losers from each round are knocked out. In a round robin tournament, each team plays every other team once, and teams that do consistently well are ranked higher. Elimination tournaments are quick, since half the teams are knocked out in each round. A round robin usually requires more rounds (one fewer than the number of teams). You can organize a simple round robin by moving all but one of the teams or players in a circle (below). Many soccer leagues use a double round robin, in which each team plays every other team home and away.

ROUND 1	ROUND 2	ROUND 3
1 2	1 3	1 4
V V	V V	V V
3 4	4 2	2 3

100-METER SPRINT RECORD IN SECONDS

1920s	10.4 (Men)	12.0 (Women)
1960s	9.95 (Men)	11.08 (Women)
2012	9.572 (Men)	10.49 (Women)

That means that training can be targeted on specific weaknesses.

In fact, without math, sports would be impossible. How would you even know that both goals on a field were the same size? Numbers can specify everything from field and court dimensions to the weight, pressure, and elasticity (bounciness) of a ball.

UM ...

PASS THE ICOSAHEDRON!

A standard soccerball isn't perfectly round. It was traditionally stitched from 32 panels—20 hexagons and 12 pentagons—and is a curved version of a solid figure called a truncated icosahedron. In 2006, a new ball with only 14 panels was introduced. But with fewer, smoother seams, the ball moved differently and—surprisingly—less predictably through the air. Ball manufacturers use mathematical models of airflow (the Navier-Stokes equations) to design new balls.

POLE VAULT RECORDS

1920s	4.30m (Men)
1960s	5.44m (Men)
1992	4.05m (First recognized women's record)
2012	6.14m (Men) 5.06m (Women)

OUCH!

LONG JUMP RECORDS

1920s	7.93m (Men)	5.98m (Women)
1960s	8.90m (Men)	6.82m (Women)
2012	8.95m (Men)	7.52m (Women)

LANGUAGE
OF THE
UNIVERSE

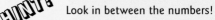
HINT! Look in between the numbers!

Math and physics are close relatives. One of the most incredible things about math—sometimes called its "unreasonable effectiveness" —is just how well it works to describe the universe. Time and again, equations from a theory in physics have predicted things that were only observed much later in experiments. It's hard to believe that you can come up with a good explanation of how the Sun shines just by fiddling around with some symbols on paper. At the subatomic scale and at the scale of the universe, it seems as if math doesn't just provide a model or description of reality, but that it really is "in" there.

So if you're thinking of the universe in terms of atoms, light, electricity, gravity, stars, space, and time, then math is definitely one language you need to know.

LAWS OF MOTION

Humans have been trying to figure out what makes things move since ancient times. Thanks to a mathematical revolution that began in the 17th century, we can now accurately send a rover on a 311-million-mile (500-million-kilometer) journey to Mars.

The ancient Greeks didn't have much of an idea about motion. They thought that heavier objects fell faster than lighter ones, for example. In the Middle Ages, Islamic mathematicians began to understand ideas like acceleration, and by the 16th century, the Italian scientist Galileo Galilei was conducting careful experiments. He timed balls rolling down ramps and dropped objects of different weights off towers. Galileo discovered the principle of inertia: An object that is at rest or moving at a constant speed remains at rest or moving at that speed, unless it is pushed by a force.

Newton's laws of motion

Force   Acceleration

1. A body continues in a state of rest or uniform motion in a straight line unless acted upon by an outside force.
2. The acceleration of an object is proportional to the force acting on it. Doubling the force of an object doubles its acceleration.
3. When one object pushes on another with a force ("action"), the second object pushes back the same amount ("reaction") in the opposite direction.

CALCULUS?

In the same book where he described the laws of motion, the British scientist Isaac Newton introduced the idea of a force that pulls together all objects with mass (matter): gravity. He backed his ideas with geometry. Newton also developed an alternative mathematical way to study motion and change, called calculus. Around the same time, the German Gottfried Leibniz independently invented calculus. This led to a bitter fight between them. Today, both are recognized as joint inventors.

Galileo is said to have dropped two cannonballs of different masses from the top of the Leaning Tower of Pisa. He wanted to prove that heavy and light objects fall at the same rate—and he was right.

Hey! Watch it!

Newton's laws

In the late 17th century, Isaac Newton took Galileo's principle of inertia and added two more "laws." Newton's second law describes how a force (push) on an object accelerates it. The third law describes how, if you push against something, it pushes back with the same force. Newton showed that these laws, and his law of gravity, were true for all objects in the universe, from falling apples to planets.

Isaac Newton

We now know that Newton's laws are very precise except at very small scales (around the size of atoms) or at very high speeds (close to the speed of light). At small scales, we need quantum mechanics, which relies on a lot of algebra. And near the speed of light, we have to explain motion using Albert Einstein's theory of relativity.

Try this at home:
Make Earth move

The ancient Greek thinker Archimedes once said, "Give me a lever long enough, and I'll move Earth." Well, finding a lever long or strong enough is tricky (so is finding a place to rest it). But you can easily make Earth move: Newton's laws say so. If you push against Earth, say by jumping up and landing with a thump, then it pushes against you (third law). These pushes make you accelerate upward—and they also make Earth accelerate downward (second law)! Of course, Earth barely moves. This is because it is much—MUCH—more massive than you are.

ORBITS

What goes up must come down—except if it escapes Earth's gravity! Newton's Law of Gravitation explains why apples fall to Earth, the shape of the Moon's orbit, and how to use a planet as a catapult.

Newton's Law of Gravitation says that every piece of matter in the universe attracts every other piece with a force called gravity. The famous story is that Newton's insight was inspired when he saw an apple fall from a tree and wondered why it fell toward the ground. Among its other effects, gravity keeps the planets orbiting the Sun and moons orbiting their planets.

A slow cannonball soon falls to Earth.

OUCH!! It's supposed to be the apple, you know!

Orbiting and escaping

Newton imagined a cannon on top of a mountain that can shoot cannonballs horizontally at any speed. At low speeds, the cannonballs fall back to Earth. If it is shot fast enough, a cannonball never hits the surface, but stays at the same height above the ground. It is then in a circular orbit around Earth. If the ball is shot with an even higher speed, it will leave Earth and shoot off into space. The speed at which this happens is called the escape velocity.

A GRAVITATIONAL SLINGSHOT

Spacecraft can use a planet's gravity like a slingshot to catapult it on at high speed. It is a little bit like it has been bounced off the planet. The *Voyager 1* probe, launched in 1977, used the gravity of the "gas giant" planets to boost its speed and head into interstellar space.

Over escape velocity, the cannonball leaves Earth's gravity.

In theory, a ball fired fast enough could go into orbit.

Black holes are objects in space with such dense gravity nothing can escape—not even light. Black holes may be created when giant stars collapse under the force of their own gravity.

The inverse square law

The strength of gravity decreases with distance, so objects that are farther apart attract each other less. If you double the distance, the force is quartered ($\frac{1}{2}^2$), and if you go three times as far, the force is only $\frac{1}{9}$th ($\frac{1}{3}^2$), so the law is called an inverse square law. This simple law is what shapes the orbits of everything in the universe.

I'm sure it should be over there!

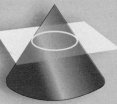
Parabola

Ellipse

Hyperbola

Geometry in space

In the 17th century, the German Johannes Kepler realized that the planets were not where they should be if their orbits were circular. He showed that the planets moved in orbits shaped like ellipses. Later, Newton proved this mathematically. Newton's laws predict that orbits are always shaped like slices through a hollow cone. When the slice is parallel to the slope of the cone, the shape is a parabola. At a shallower angle, the shape is an ellipse or circle. At steeper angles, the shape is a hyperbola. Parabolic and hyperbolic orbits are "open"— the ends don't join up. A comet visiting our solar system might have a hyperbolic orbit around the Sun: It swings around close to the Sun and leaves, never to be seen again.

TIME

Without time, there would be no change—no growth, no movement, no life. Though it's hard to define, we all think we understand how time passes. But modern physics shows that time is much stranger than you think.

Humans first recorded the passing of time by counting sunrises, moon phases, and seasons. The invention of mechanical clocks meant that we could measure very short periods of time. This allowed scientists to make precise observations.

Try this at home:
How to draw time

You'll need a shopping cart, a plastic bottle, and a smooth surface. Prick a hole in the base of the bottle and seal it with tape. Fill the bottle with water, or sand, and tie it to the cart so it can swing freely with the hole pointing down. Remove the tape and swing the bottle from side to side. Push the cart steadily forward. As the bottle swings, the water or sand draws a shape called a sine wave. Sine waves appear in sound waves, light, radio waves, and even ocean waves.

Keeping time

Clocks keep time by counting a steady vibration or oscillation, such as a swinging pendulum. Today, most watches and clocks count the vibrations of a tiny tuning fork made from quartz crystal. When quartz is connected to a battery, it vibrates and sends electrical pulses at a precise frequency (rate). Usually, the crystal is shaped so that it vibrates 32,768, or 2^{15} times a second. An electronic circuit adds these pulses to get a "tick" every second. Quartz clocks can be accurate to 5 seconds a year. The most accurate clocks, atomic clocks, count the vibrations of electrons within atoms. They can be accurate to one 100-millionth of a second each year.

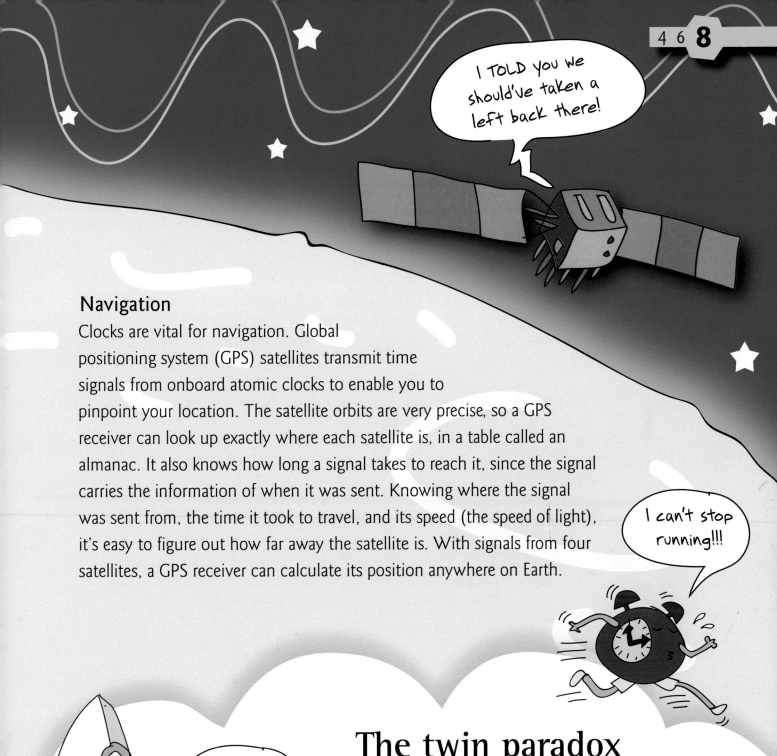

Navigation

Clocks are vital for navigation. Global positioning system (GPS) satellites transmit time signals from onboard atomic clocks to enable you to pinpoint your location. The satellite orbits are very precise, so a GPS receiver can look up exactly where each satellite is, in a table called an almanac. It also knows how long a signal takes to reach it, since the signal carries the information of when it was sent. Knowing where the signal was sent from, the time it took to travel, and its speed (the speed of light), it's easy to figure out how far away the satellite is. With signals from four satellites, a GPS receiver can calculate its position anywhere on Earth.

The twin paradox

In the early 20th century, Albert Einstein's theories of relativity changed the idea of time. His special theory of relativity says that clocks run at different speeds, depending on how fast they're traveling, while the general theory says that time is slowed by gravity. At the top of a skyscraper, where Earth's gravity is slightly less strong than at the bottom, clocks run a little bit faster than clocks at the bottom. If an astronaut traveled for years near the speed of light, she would return to Earth to find that her twin had aged many years, while she remained young.

THE ULTIMATE SPEED LIMIT

Clocks slowing down and people shrinking as they travel faster. Sounds crazy, but it's all down to the speed of light.

What happened to you?

The flight arrived early!

When you turn on a lamp, how long does it take for the light to reach your eyes? It seems to be instant. Light isn't that fast—but it is the fastest thing in the universe. In a vacuum (empty space) the speed of light, called c, is about 186,000 miles (300,000km) per second. Light from the Sun takes about 8 minutes to reach us, and light from the next nearest star takes more than 4 years. When you look at the Andromeda galaxy, you're seeing ancient history—the light left it 2.5 million years ago!

Relativity

In the 17th century, Galileo came up with a "principle of relativity." If you are below deck on a smoothly sailing ship, he said, and can't see out, there's no experiment you can do (like dropping a ball) to tell if you are moving or standing still. You need to see another object to check.

Newton added to this the idea that time flowed at the same speed everywhere in the universe. With Galileo's principle and Newton's laws, you can add speeds in an obvious way. If a friend passes you on a skateboard at 5 meters per second (m/s) and throws a ball in the same direction at 10 m/s, you can measure the ball's speed as 15 m/s (5 + 10).

Ow! Too fast!

OUCH!

They told me I only needed a yard!

Crazy but true

In 1905, Albert Einstein corrected Newton's ideas with his special theory of relativity. This starts from the idea that speed of light is the same for everyone, whether moving or standing still. The effects of special relativity are tiny at low speeds, but large near the speed of light. Take your friend on the skateboard. If she zooms past at 90 percent the speed of light and throws a ball at the same speed in the same direction, the ball will travel at about 99 percent of the speed of light—not 180 percent. As she travels faster, her watch ticks slower, and she gets smaller in the direction of travel—and heavier. Relativity also says that the mass and energy of an object are related:

E (energy) $= mc^2$ (mass x speed of light squared).

SPECIAL EFFECTS

Relativity has some strange effects. If a car drove past you at a speed close to the speed of light, it would seem to shrink in size. And a yardstick on a high-speed alien ship would look short to you as it whizzed past—but if you were also holding a yardstick (yes, we know it's unlikely, but then so is the alien in the spaceship), your ruler would look short to the alien. That's relativity! But if you and the alien both measured the speed of light, you'd get exactly the same result.

It's unhealthy to break the speed limit: The special theory of relativity says that a car contracts in length as it nears the speed of light.

0% of c

0 mi./s (0km/s)
Car length at rest

66% of c

442 million mph (712 million km/h)
The car travels around Earth in a second

99% of c

0.66 million mph (1.06 million km/h)
The car travels around Earth 7.5 times in a second

SHAPE OF THE UNIVERSE

What shape is space? Does it stretch to infinity in all directions? And what do physicists mean when they say it has four dimensions ... or even 10?

When we want to fix a point in space, we use three coordinates: height, length, and depth. For many years, people thought that space and time were unrelated. But in 1908, mathematician Hermann Minkowski came up with the idea of "space-time," combining the three dimensions of space with one of time. Every event can be "located" using four coordinates, three for where it is and one for when.

The idea of space-time helps with understanding Einstein's theory of special relativity. Special relativity has a new idea of distance between two events in the universe, which involves time as well as space. And space-time was vital for Einstein's theory of gravity, called general relativity.

Isaac Newton thought of gravity as a force that makes objects fall to the ground or holds planets in their orbit. But Einstein thought of gravity in a different way—as a bending of space-time.

More than four!

Physicists think that instead of just three dimensions of space, there may be 10 or more. In one theory called string theory, the universe has 10 dimensions of space and one of time. These extra dimensions are curled up so tightly that we can't travel to them, and they only have an effect on subatomic particles (the minute particles that are inside an atom).

And how is this scientific?!!

HIDDEN DIMENSIONS

For something as big as a human, this rope is a one-dimensional object. You can say exactly where you are on it with just one number—the distance from the end of the rope—and the two tightrope walkers can't pass each other. For the ants, the rope is a two-dimensional object (the other dimension is how far around the circumference they are). They can easily pass each other by moving aside.

Think of space-time as a stretched rubber sheet, like a trampoline. A massive object such as a star distorts (warps) space-time, just like a heavy ball on a stretched rubber sheet makes a dip in the sheet. The movement of smaller objects nearby is affected by the dip. This distortion is gravity. In space, the planets roll around the dip created by a star, and even light is bent by it.

The shape of space

Current theories say that on a small scale (say, the size of our solar system, which is tiny in space terms), the universe is pretty flat, but it used to be tiny and tightly curved. As for its size, from Earth we can see to the edges of a sphere 90 billion light years across. The universe is probably much bigger than this—and it's still expanding.

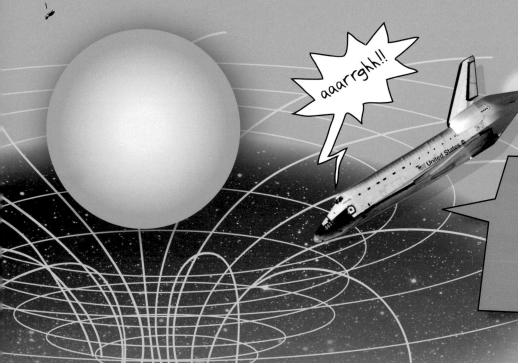

Warps in space-time might be created by objects with massive gravity such as black holes. But they're way too far from Earth to interrupt space travel ... yet.

PROBLEM SOLVED!

Pages 20–21 Unfeasibly large numbers
The board holds a total of $2^{64} - 1$ pennies, or
18,446,744,073,709,551,615.

Pages 22–23 An infinity of infinities
Hilbert's hotel can accommodate a countable infinity of arrivals by moving the original guests to the rooms numbered twice their original room. The guest in room 1 moves to room 2, the guest in room 2 to room 4, and so on. Now the original guests are in the infinitely many even-numbered rooms, and the new arrivals can move into the (infinitely many) odd-numbered rooms.

Pages 24–25 The prime numbers
Euler's prime formula works for all numbers from 1 to 40, but $41^2 + 41 + 41$ is not prime (it can be divided by 41).

Pages 28–29 Sets and logic
Hat trick solution: Both A and B could be orange, both could be green, or one could be orange and one green. If both were orange, then C would be certain that her hat was green (since there are only two orange hats in the bag). But if at least one of A and B is green, then C could be either orange or green. So after C's answer, A and B know that at least one of them has a green hat. If A were orange, then B would have to be green (since one of them must have a green hat), but if A were green, then B wouldn't know his color. Once B admits he doesn't know his hat color, A can tell that her own hat is green.
Venn diagram solution: Group 1 liked neither zebras nor rhinos.

Pages 30–31 Proofs
The number 2 is prime and it's even, so you've found a counterexample that disproves the statement.

Pages 46–47 Graphs and networks
It's impossible to draw a line from each house to each utility company without the lines crossing—at least, if you draw it on a flat piece of paper. It IS possible to do this on a torus. Here's one way:

Pages 70–71 Keeping secrets
The quick brown fox jumps over the lazy dog.
(This is a pangram—a sentence that contains all the letters of the alphabet.)

NUMBER SEQUENCES
Chapter 1 has two sequences.
1, 4, 9, 16, 25 ... These are the first five square numbers ($1^2 = 1$, $2^2 = 4$, $3^2 = 9$, etc.).

1, 3, 6, 10, 15, 21 ... These are the first six triangular numbers:

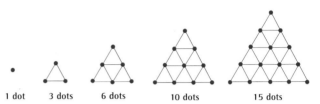

1 dot   3 dots   6 dots   10 dots   15 dots

Chapter 2
1, 2, 4, 8, 16, 31, 57 ...
A very tricky one, to show that sequences don't always continue as expected. This is the number of pieces a circle is divided into when 1, 2, 3, 4 ... points on its circumference are joined by straight lines, so that at most, 2 cross each other.

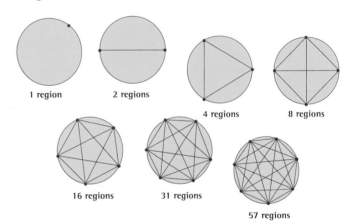

1 region   2 regions   4 regions   8 regions
16 regions   31 regions   57 regions

Chapter 3
9, 3, 1, 1/3, 1/9 ... Each number is the previous one divided by 3.

Chapter 4
1, 3, 4, 7, 11, 18, 29, 47, 76, 123 ...
These are the Lucas numbers. They're just like the Fibonacci numbers, with each number being the sum of the previous two, except that the sequence starts with 1, 3 rather than 1, 1.

Chapter 5
4, 6, 8, 9, 10 ...
These are the composite (nonprime) numbers. The pattern is easier to spot if you consider which numbers are missing.

BIOGRAPHIES

Albert EINSTEIN (1879–1955)

Einstein's early ambition was to teach math and physics, but he ended up working as a technical officer at a patent office in Switzerland. In his spare time, he wrote the scientific papers that even today are the best descriptions we have of how the universe works at large scales. Although his work contains the seeds of the idea of the atom bomb, he later campaigned for peace and against nuclear weapons.

Paul ERDÖS (1913–1996)

The Hungarian Paul Erdös was devoted to solving mathematical problems. Most of the time, he didn't have a permanent job or even a home; he traveled around with a few possessions in a suitcase, searching for people to work with. He wrote more than 1,500 papers about prime numbers, graph theory, and combinatorics. When Erdös was awarded a $50,000 prize, he used most of it to set up a prize fund for other mathematicians.

Philippa FAWCETT (1868–1948)

In 1909, women weren't even allowed to be awarded degrees at Cambridge University in England, but Fawcett scored top marks in the school's math exams. Newspapers around the world reported the event and said it proved that women were just as capable as men, even in mathematics. After teaching at Cambridge, Fawcett worked to reorganize the education systems in South Africa and England.

Pierre de FERMAT (1601–1665)

Fermat trained as a lawyer and became interested in math in his late 20s. Fermat famously claimed that you couldn't find nonzero integers x, y, and z that solved the equation $x^n + y^n = z^n$ for n bigger than 2. He said he had a "truly remarkable proof," but no room to write it down. Fermat's Last Theorem remained unproved for over 300 years, until 1994.

Evariste GALOIS (1811–1832)

Born in France, Galois wrote his first mathematical research paper while still at school. Although brilliant, he couldn't get along with academic systems and wasn't recognized for his ideas in his lifetime. He was imprisoned for his political activities and persuaded to take part in a duel, in which he was killed. Galois's ideas about solving equations created a whole field of math called Galois Theory. He was only 21 when he died.

John von NEUMANN (1903–1957)

The Hungarian-born von Neumann was so good at math that he flew through university math exams while actually studying something else (chemistry). A true genius, he worked alongside Einstein in the United States in the 1930s. He changed many different areas of math. The architecture (internal circuits) of modern computers owes a lot to his ideas. He had such a powerful mind that he couldn't work without distraction: He needed the TV on full blast! He was also famous for throwing wild parties.

Amalie Emmy NOETHER (1882–1935)

Although she was an outstanding mathematician, the German Emmy Noether had a difficult career. Women were not allowed in many universities, and despite the support of leading mathematicians, Noether didn't get official recognition until the last years of her life. Noether is famous for her work in algebra, and her ideas helped Einstein's general theory of relativity.

Henri POINCARÉ (1854–1912)

Poincaré worked across many areas of math and physics, including the notorious three-body problem (understanding the orbits of three planets or stars that feel each other's gravitational pull), special relativity (Einstein's theory), and the beginnings of chaos theory.

Alan TURING (1912–1954)

Alan Turing is best known for his ideas of the Turing Machine, a theoretical computer, and the Turing Test, which is designed to tell if a machine is "intelligent." These ideas grew in importance years later as computers and artificial intelligence became a practical reality. During World War II, Turing was involved in breaking the German Enigma code.

Andrew WILES (1953–)

When he was 10 years old, British mathematician Wiles read about Fermat's Last Theorem. He was amazed that the question was so simple that he could understand it, yet no one had solved it. In 1993, he claimed to have proved the theorem. But other mathematicians found a mistake in his working. Wiles struggled to fix it and almost gave up when, a year later, he unexpectedly found a solution. Wiles's proof uses modern ideas: If Fermat really did have a proof, it must have been very different.

GLOSSARY

acceleration A measure of how much faster (or slower) something travels in each second.

algebra The part of math that deals with solving equations, but also with the "structure" (internal shape) of and relationships between mathematical ideas and objects.

angle The shape formed where two lines meet at a point. Angles are commonly measured in degrees, but in math they are sometimes measured in radians: 360 degrees = 2π radians.

arithmetic The part of math dealing with calculations, especially those involving integers.

complex number A number pair, made up of a real number and an imaginary number.

composite A natural number greater than 1 that is not prime. Note that 1 is neither prime nor composite.

conjecture A statement that seems to be true but has not yet been proved. Once a statement has been proved, it is called a theorem.

coordinate In two dimensions (e.g. on a map), coordinates are numbers (such as 1, 5) that fix your distance away from an origin, along two directions. In three dimensions, you need three coordinates to fix a position.

cube number (or perfect cube) A cube number is one that equals an integer multiplied by itself twice. The number 64 is a cube because $64 = 4 \times 4 \times 4$.

distance A basic property of a space. Distance is a measure between two points in space.

equation A statement written in symbols and containing an equals sign, in which the right-hand side is the same as the left-hand side. Equations contain things that are known and others that are unknown. In $x + 7 = 11$, x is unknown, and there is only one solution: $x = 4$.

equilateral A regular triangle, with three equal sides and three equal angles.

factorize To break down a number into the numbers that were multiplied to produce it.

finite Not infinite.

fraction Part of a whole. Fractions are rational numbers.

geometry The mathematical study of shapes.

imaginary number The square root of a negative number. $\sqrt{-1}$ is called i, and all other imaginary numbers are multiples of i. For example, $\sqrt{-49}$ is $7i$, and $\sqrt{-1/4} = 1/2\,i$.

infinite Without limit. Infinity is not a number, and you can't do arithmetic with it. There are different sizes of infinities: There are infinitely many natural numbers and infinitely many real numbers, but there are many more real numbers than natural numbers!

integer The set of integers is the set of all natural numbers (1, 2, 3 ...), their negatives (–1, –2, –3 ...), and zero.

irrational number A real number that cannot be written as a ratio between an integer and a natural number—for example, $\sqrt{2}$ or π. The digits in the decimal expression for an irrational number go on forever, with no periodic pattern.

line In math, a line is defined as a one-dimensional shape that has zero width and infinite length. Lines and points are the basic objects of geometry.

model A mathematical model is a "picture" of the real world using equations. A good model explains observations and predicts what will happen, accurately.

natural number A positive counting number: 1, 2, 3 ... There are infinitely many natural numbers. Sometimes, zero is thought of as a natural number.

negative Less than zero. Zero is neither positive nor negative.

notation Symbols and rules for combining them. Math used to be written with lots of words; now it's written with a lot of symbols. New ideas often need new notation, and new notation can help spark new ideas.

operation (binary operation) A binary operation takes two numbers and produces one number. The operations of arithmetic are addition, subtraction, multiplication, and division.

perfect number A number that equals the sum of its proper divisors, e.g. 6 has proper divisors 1, 2, and 3, and $6 = 1 + 2 + 3$.

periodic Repeating in a regular way. A pendulum's swing and the vibrations of a guitar string are periodic.

plane A plane is a flat surface that goes on forever in every direction.

point In math, a point is a zero-dimensional object (without length, area, or volume). Points and lines are the basic objects of geometry.

polygon A plane (flat), closed figure with straight sides. Triangles, quadrilaterals, and pentagons are all polygons.

polyhedron A three-dimensional, closed figure with faces made of polygons. There are only five regular convex polyhedra, called the Platonic solids: the tetrahedron (triangular-based pyramid), cube, octahedron, icosahedron, and dodecahedron.

positive Greater than zero. Zero is neither positive nor negative.

prime A natural number greater than 1 that can only be divided by itself and 1. *See* composite.

product The result you get when you multiply numbers.

quadrilateral A polygon with four sides. All rectangles are quadrilaterals, though not all quadrilaterals are rectangles.

random Unpredictable. The score you get when you throw a fair die is random.

ratio The ratio of two numbers is a fraction with one written as the numerator and the other as the denominator. The ratio of 3 and 5 is 3/5.

rational number A number that can be written as a ratio between an integer divided by any other integer except zero.

real number A number that is found along the continuous number line. The real numbers are all the rationals and all the irrationals taken together.

regular (figure) A shape whose sides and angles are all identical. A square is a regular quadrilateral.

remainder What is left over when an integer can't be divided exactly by another. For example, $10 \div 3 = 3$ remainder 1.

sequence A sequence is a list of numbers in an order, e.g. 1, 2, 3, 2, 1. Each number in a sequence is called a term. Sequences can be infinitely long. In an arithmetic sequence, a fixed number is added to each term to get the next term, eg. 1, 5, 9, 13 … In a geometric sequence, each term is multiplied by a fixed number to get the next term, eg. 1, 5, 25, 125 …

set A collection of things called elements. An element can be anything, even another set. The order of the elements in a set doesn't matter. A set with no elements is called the empty set, symbol $\emptyset$.

space A place with certain properties, including a number of dimensions (two for a plane, three for a solid figure, etc.).

speed Distance traveled divided by time taken. Velocity is a speed in a particular direction.

square number (or perfect square) A square number is one that equals an integer multiplied by itself. The number 64 is square because $64 = 8 \times 8$.

square root The square root of a number is the number that, when multiplied by itself, gives the original number. The square root of 9 is 3 because $3^2 = 3 \times 3 = 9$. Every number apart from zero has two square roots: a positive and a negative one.

subset A set of things that is included in a bigger set.

sum The result when you add numbers.

surface A space with two dimensions only, meaning it takes just two numbers to fix a position anywhere on it. A plane is a surface, but surfaces can also be curved, like a sphere, or even more complicated.

surface area The "amount" of a surface. The greater the area, the more paint is needed to cover it.

velocity Speed in a given direction. Two objects moving at the same speed but in different directions have different velocities.

volume The amount of space that a solid takes up.

whole number Usually, a natural number—though sometimes, the word is used to mean an integer.

RESOURCES

The two best online math resources are Wikipedia and Wolfram's Mathworld.
http://mathworld.wolfram.com/
Wikipedia articles usually have much more explanation than the Mathworld ones, but even so, they can be tough. An easier place to start is the Simple Wikipedia:
http://simple.wikipedia.org/wiki/Mathematics

The only way to really understand math is by doing it, through exploring math games and puzzles. Try one of **Marilyn Burns'** books (such as *I Hate Mathematics*) first and then move on to the fantastic **Martin Gardner**. Although not a professional mathematician, Gardner wrote a column on math games and puzzles in *Scientific American* magazine for 25 years and exchanged ideas with some of the best mathematicians around.

Other authors whose work you should definitely check out are **Keith Devlin**, **Douglas Hofstadter**, and **Ian Stewart**. Hofstadter's *Gödel, Escher, Bach* is brilliant, but don't expect to understand it all at once! **Timothy Gowers** has written a small book called *Mathematics: A Very Short Introduction* that you could also try dipping into.

You shouldn't expect to be able to read any of these books from cover to cover—but you can learn some incredible math from any of them in just a few pages.

INDEX